ENGLISH LANGUAGE MASTERMIND:

From

Confident Communication

To

Higher Test Scores

- by Everett Ofori

© Everett Ofori, 2018

All rights reserved. No part of this publication may be reproduced, stored in a retrieval system, or transmitted, in any form or by any means, without the prior permission in writing of Everett Ofori, or as expressly permitted by law, or under terms agreed with the appropriate reprographics rights organization.

Enquiries concerning reproduction outside the scope of the above should be sent to:

Everett Ofori
c/o Takarazuka University of Art and Design
Tokyo Campus Building 1F-123MBE
7-11-1 Nishi-Shinjuku
Shinjuku-ku
Tokyo, Japan 160-0023

10-digit ISBN: 1-894221-16-18
13-digit ISBN: 978-1-894221-16-0

Other Books by Everett Ofori

Succeeding From the Margins of Canadian Society:
A Strategic Resource for New Immigrants, Refugees
and International Students
Written by Francis Adu-Febiri and Everett Ofori
© 2009 – ISBN 978-1-926585-27-7

Read Assure: Guaranteed Formula for Reading Success with Phonics
Written by Everett Ofori
© 2010 – ISBN 978-1-926585-83-3

Guaranteed Formula for Writing Success
Written by Everett Ofori
© 2011 – ISBN 978-1-926918-22-8

The Changing Japanese Woman: From Yamatonadeshiko to YamatonadeGucci
Written by Everett Ofori
© 2013 – ISBN 10: 1894221044
ISBN 13: 978-1894221047

Prepare for Greatness: How to Make Your Success Inevitable
Written by Everett Ofori
© 2013 – ISBN 10: 0921143001
ISBN 13: 978-0921143000

The Global Student's Companion:
10,001 Timeless Themes & Topics for Dialogue, Discussion & Debate Practice
Compiled by Everett Ofori
© 2015 – ISBN 10: 1-894221-02-8
ISBN 13: 978-1-894221-02-3

Guaranteed Formula for Effective Business Writing
Written by Everett Ofori
© 2011 – ISBN 978-1894221108

Table of Contents

Introduction		8
	Purposeful Reading Template	10
STEP 1	Graded Readers	11
STEP 2	What Good English Communicators Read	12
	Magazines & Newspapers	13
STEP 3	Improving Your Listening Skills	16
	Listen & Write Practice Template	18
STEP 4	The Road to Reading Riches	21
STEP 5	Verbs - #1	24
STEP 6	Homonyms - #1	28
STEP 7	Verb Tenses - #1	41
STEP 8	Quick Response Practice	51
STEP 9	Word Forms - #1 (Verbs, Nouns, Adjectives)	52
STEP 10	Homonyms - #2	58
STEP 11	Word Forms - #2 (Verbs, Nouns, Adjectives)	66
STEP 12	Verbs - #2	79
STEP 13	Know Your Prepositions	84
STEP 14	Preposition Combinations	91
STEP 15	Common Occupations	96
STEP 16	By versus Until	102
STEP 17	Word Forms - #3: Nouns and their Verbs	105
STEP 18	Verbs followed by Gerunds	111
STEP 19	Go, Play, or Do?	116
STEP 20	Verbs followed by Infinitives	119

STEP 21	Focus on Nouns	123
STEP 22	Word Forms - #4 (Nouns, Verbs, Adjectives)	130
STEP 23	Verbs followed by Gerunds or Infinitives	134
STEP 24	Subject - Verb Agreement	140
STEP 25	Idiomatic Expressions - #1	143
STEP 26	Word Forms - #5 (Nouns, Verbs, Adjectives)	148
STEP 27	Transitive and Intransitive Verbs	152
STEP 28	Verbs - #3	158
STEP 29	Participial Adjectives - #1 Are you Boring or Just Bored?	161
STEP 30	Word Forms - #6 (Nouns, Verbs, Adjectives)	165
STEP 31	Verb Tenses #2	171
STEP 32	Idiomatic Expressions - #2	177
STEP 33	Prepositional Phrases	183
STEP 34	Word Forms - # 5 (Nouns, Verbs, Adjectives)	185
STEP 35	Participial Adjectives - #2	194
STEP 36	House & Home	199
STEP 37	Verb Tenses - #3	205
STEP 38	Word Forms - #8 (Nouns, Verbs, Adjectives)	209
STEP 39	More Prepositional Phrases	217
STEP 40	Prefixes - #1	221
STEP 41	Verb Tenses - #4	226
STEP 42	Word Forms - #9 (Nouns, Verbs, Adjectives)	229
STEP 43	Even More Prepositional Phrases	233
STEP 44	Suffixes - #1	235
STEP 45	More Transitive Verbs	241

STEP 46	Prefixes - #2.	245
STEP 47	Numbers Plus	251
STEP 48	Suffixes - #2.	255
STEP 49	Prefixes - #3.	261
STEP 50	Collective Nouns & Group Words - #1	267
STEP 51	Verb Tenses - #5	270
STEP 52	Word Forms - #10 (Nouns, Verbs, Adjectives)	275
STEP 53	Idiomatic Expressions - #3	283
STEP 54	Suffixes - #3.	290
STEP 55	Prefixes - #4.	296
STEP 56	Still More Prepositional Phrases	301
STEP 57	Collective Nouns & Group Words - #2.	304
STEP 58	Prefixes - #5	307
STEP 59	Suffixes - #4.	312
STEP 60	Collective Nouns & Group Words - #3.	317
STEP 61	Affixes	320
STEP 62	Idiomatic Expressions - #4	325
STEP 63	The Subjunctive.	330
STEP 64	Words & Their Connections	333
STEP 65	Word Forms - #11 (Nouns, Verbs, & Adjectives	340
STEP 66	Adjectives - #1 The Comparative & the Superlative	344
STEP 67	Transitive Verbs	349
STEP 68	Prefixes & Suffixes.	354
STEP 69	Articles: A, An, The	361
STEP 70	Adjectives - #2	377
STEP 71	Adjectives - #3	382
STEP 72	Postpositive Adjectives	406
STEP 73	Multiple Adjectives: Order	409
STEP 74	Absolute adjectives.	412
STEP 75	Adverbs - #1	418

STEP 76	Let's Get Physical	436
STEP 77	Adverbs - #2	443
STEP 78	Adjectives - #4	447
STEP 79	Let's Get Medical	461
STEP 80	Idiomatic Expressions - #4	476
STEP 81	Adjectives - #5	481
STEP 82	Let's Get Legal	494
STEP 83	Adverbs - #3	499
STEP 84	Let's Get Scientific	507
STEP 85	Adjectives - #5	515
STEP 86	Words Relating to Women	529
STEP 87	Words Relating to Men	534
STEP 88	Let's Get Athletic	540
STEP 89	Words Relating to Travel	548
STEP 90	Let's Get Academic	559
STEP 91	Phrases Galore: Sentence Writing Practice -#1	569
STEP 92	Sentence Writing Practice -#2	572
STEP 93	Sentence Writing Practice -#3	574
STEP 94	Sentence Writing Practice -#4	578
STEP 95	Sentence Writing Practice -#5	581
STEP 96	Sentence Writing Practice -#6	584
STEP 97	Sentence Writing Practice -#7	587
STEP 98	Sentence Writing Practice -#8	590
STEP 99	Sentence Writing Practice -#9	593
STEP 100	Sentence Writing Practice -#10	596
About the Author		599
Notes		600

Introduction

Each year, thousands of people struggle to increase their English test scores, be it TOEIC (Test of English for International Commmunication), TOEFL (Test of English as a Foreign Language), IELTS (The International English Language Testing System), or BULATS (Business Language Testing Service). Some succeed. Many do not. Some even regress. So, if your current study method has not been working well for you, maybe, it's time to consider another way.

You might have heard the saying, "If you always do what you've always done, you will always get what you've always got." Maybe, it's time to change change your approach.

The other way that I am suggesting is not necessarily the most popular way. But, for those who have been willing to try it, the results have often been spectacular.

In fairness, some of those who choose to study mainly by means of traditional test-preparation guides sometimes improve their scores, but at times, their higher score is not reflected in their communication skills. There must be a better way. And there is.

This book suggests following the path of native English speakers who are known to be good communicators. In fact, being a native English speaker is no guarantee that one would speak impeccable English. It is not difficult to find native speakers who would rather "conversate" than converse or those who call for "a apple" rather than an apple.

But there is one simple element that is common to virtually all English speakers who are known to be good communicators whether it's Bill Gates, Oprah Winfrey, Nelson Mandela, or Tony Robbins: THEY READ!!!

So, let's take 100 steps towards English Proficiency. It is hard work, and it takes a two-pronged approach. One part involves incessant reading and listening and the other part involves assiduously doing the exercises in this manual and having an instructor review your work.

Templates

Two templates have been provided for you below.

1) The Purposeful Reading Template (page 10) is meant for you to record new words, idioms, or expressions you pick up while reading articles, fiction, or nonfiction. Feel free to photocopy the templates and use them as often as possible. When you find new words, check their meanings, note the part of speech, that is, whether the wod is a noun, adjective, verb, or otherwise. If the word has several meanings, be sure to take note of all of them. Furthermore, look for the synonyms and antonyms of any new words you encounter. This will help you to enlarge your vocabulary substantially. Also, pay attention to new expressions and idioms you come across. Look for their meanings as well.

If you cannot find an expression in a dictionary, do an open Google search. A lot of dictionaries these days, including Longman and Cambridge, include idioms and expressions, by the way.

Please pay attention to the multiple meanings of words and expressions so that you can apply the proper meaning to the situation at hand.

2) The Listen & Write Practice Template (page 18) is meant for you to practice listening. Each listening session ought to involve listening to the same material two, three times, or four times. While listening, write down as many words as you can understand. When you finish, doublecheck the spelling of the words from your dictionary. If there is a word you do not understand, check the meaning.

Later on, listen to the same material again. While listening, write down as many words as you can make out. Compare the second list with the first list. Were you able to make out more words?

Do this kind of listening exercise everyday. Even 10 minutes a day of this exercise will help, but of course, if you are truly serious, you will devote a little more time than that.

Purposeful Reading Template

1) Title (Book/Article):
Source/Author/Date:
Word/Idiom/Expression:
Meaning (1):
Meaning (2):
Meaning (3):
Synonyms:
Antonyms:
Sample sentence::
My sentence:

2) Title (Book/Article):
Source/Author/Date:
Word/Idiom/Expression:
Meaning (1):
Meaning (2):
Meaning (3):
Synonyms:
Antonyms:
Sample sentence::
My sentence:

STEP 1

Graded Readers

For beginning English learners, graded readers are very useful because they start with easy vocabulary and gradually increase the number of words as the reader moves up to the higher reading grades. This can make reading comfortable for the unsure beginner.

Some graded readers are only a few pages, and some run to twenty or thirty pages, but they are written in a way that makes reading joyful.

If you make it a habit of reading one graded reader every week, or every couple of weeks, you'll be amazed at how much progress you'll make. Some who have started with level one books have been surprised to learn from those books things they never learned in their English textbooks. A new world awaits!

If you're in the mood for shopping for graded readers, here are a few companies you might consider:

- Atama-ii Books
- Helbling languages
- Cambridge University Press
- Cengage/Heinle
- Compass Media
- e-future ELT
- Penguin Readers
- MPI
- Express Publishing
- R.I.C. Publications
- Ladybird (Penguin)
- Macmillan Readers
- McGraw Hill Asia
- MM Publications
- Pearson English Readers
- Matsuka Phonics Institute
- Scholastic ELT
- Burlington Books
- Richmond Publishing
- Penguin ELT
- Garnet Education
- Black Cat - Cideb

These books can be found at any major bookstore or through online purchase.

STEP 2

What Good English Communicators Read

If you read for fun and for knowledge, you become accustomed to the flow of the language. Eventually, you get to the point where you can predict what words or phrases are coming up ahead.

Extensive reading is also another way to acquire knowledge of grammar. Those who read books and articles written with care, consciously or unconsciously, form the habit of communicating in grammatically correct English. Please keep this in mind as you build skills toward native English level proficiency.

How Children Learn Language
Children learn to communicate by getting INPUT from their surroundings: their parents, relatives, family friends, teachers, schoolmates and the whole range of people who come in contact with the child. If a child has parents who speak correctly and insist on accuracy, the child is likely to acquire similar habits of communication. But if you are learning English in an environment where there are not many English speakers, how can you get the input necessary for you to communicate well? The answer is books! Most great books go through an editing process, so that the material you end up reading is of fairly good quality. If you consistently get the benefit of such input, it is going to have an impact on your own communication skills. And, if you are not happy about your reading fluency, make use of phonics, which is arguably the best way to learn to read fluently in English. There are many phonics books and online resources to help you improve your reading. Take advantage of them.

From the next page, you will find a list of newspapers and magazines that good English communicators read on a daily or weekly basis. Check them out.

Magazines & Newspapers

	For Beginners/Low Level Learners
1	Time for Kids
2	KidsPost – The Washington Post *For Beginners/Low level*
3	Voice of America *For Beginners/Low level*
4	Young Post – South China Morning Post *For Beginners/Low level*
	For Intermediate to Advanced Level Learners
5	LearnEnglish
6	Forbes
7	Business Insider
8	BloombergBusinessweek
9	The Wall Street Journal
10	CNBC
11	Market Watch
12	International Business Times
13	Entrepreneur
14	Inc.
15	Seeking Alpha
16	Economist
17	Fortune
18	Harvard Business Review
19	Business Journals
20	Coindesk
21	Fast Company
22	TheStreet
23	FOX Business
24	Business Daily News
25	Kiplinger
26	Business2Community
27	Insidermonkey
28	Global Banking & Finance Review
29	Investors.com
30	Barron's
31	Success

32	Advertising Age
33	ValueWalk
34	24/7 Wall St
35	Fast Co.
36	Global Financial Marketing Review
37	BenZinga
38	Business.com
39	The Fiscal Times
40	4-Traders
41	Inman News - Real Estate
42	Marketplace
43	Strategy+Business
44	Investment News
45	Black Enterprise
46	American Banker
47	PE Hub
48	Equities.com
49	Financial Planning
50	Selling Power
51	Minyanville
52	Bloomberg View
53	Insurance News Net
54	International Finance Magazine
55	Traders
56	Worth
57	CNNMoney
58	MSN Money
59	Yahoo! Finance
60	Google Finance
61	Bloomberg Markets
62	Money
63	The Globe and Mail
64	HuffPost
65	Straits Times (Singapore)
66	BBC
67	The Guardian
68	The Japan Times
69	The Vancouver Sun
70	Sydney Morning Herald
71	Profit (Canada)

72	Canadian Business
73	The Canadian Business Journal
74	ProfitGuide
75	Maclean's
76	Knowledge@Wharton
77	INSEAD Knowledge
78	Wealth Creator
79	Financial Review
80	Money Magazine
81	Smart Investor
82	Australian Property Investor
83	Marketing
84	Your Trading Edge (YTE)
85	Australian Business Solutions magazine
86	The Motley Fool
87	The Los Angeles Times
88	The Chicago Tribune
89	Crain's Detroit News
90	National Post (Canada)
91	Calgary Herald (Canada)
92	Edmonton Journal (Canada)
93	Times Colonist (Canada)
94	The Montreal Gazette (Canada)
95	The London Free Press (Canada)
96	Business Matters
97	Advertising World (UK)
98	African Business (UK)
99	Marketing Week (UK)
100	Enterprise Magazine (UK)

This is just a sampling of the wide range of newspapers and magazines available for your reading pleasure. If you devote some time to doing a search online, you will discover many more gems.

STEP 3
Improving Your Listening Skills

In Japan and elsewhere in Asia, it is quite common to see English learners on trains, in coffee shops, and parks, listening intently to their English audio lessons while following along in their accompanying textbook.

It is easy to appreciate the dedication of such students, listening to lessons day in and day out. But some of these students do not see huge improvements in their communication ability despite putting in so much effort. Why is this?

Part of the answer may lie in research that has been conducted on babies and their language acquisition potential. When researchers played CDs with human voices to babies, they could detect minimal baby brain activity..

On the other hand, when babies heard the human voice directly, their brains lighted up immediately. It seems that babies are wired ready to benefit from the social interaction with other human beings.

If you listen passively to an audio lesson, there is definitely a benefit, but maybe the benefit is minimal. Watching television passively is no different.

Consider, however, children who watch comedians on TV and try to imitate the comedians. Pretty soon, they become little comedians themselves. The little comedians are successful because they did not listen passively to their favorite comedian. They imitated the comedian. They tried to say or sing or play like the comedian. And there lies the secret of their success.

Instead of listening passively to your audio materials, if you will be like the little comedian and try to shadow what you are listening to, your success will be much swifter because your mind will be much more engaged.

Listen & Write

An even more active way to improve your listening skills is to listen and write. If it sounds difficult, it is because it is! But, the effort will pay off if you are willing to persist in the practice. Here is how it works:

1) Choose a podcast (something you can play again)
2) Take a blank piece of paper.
3) Grab a pen
4) As soon as you begin playing the podcast, write down as many words as you can catch and keep going until the podcast ends. This can include individual words, phrases, or even sentences. After the podcast ends, check to see that all the words you wrote down can be found in the dictionary. If there are any new or unfamiliar words, check their meanings. This will also improve your spelling.
5) Count the total number of words you were able to catch.
6) The first time you do this, your total word count might be low. That's all right.
7) Play the podcast again, and once more, try to write down as many words, phrases or sentences as you can.
8) Did you pick up any other new words? If so, check to see that they are in the dictionary and that you understand exactly what they mean.
9) Do this every day.

Note: Please see the next page for a listening practice template

Listen & Write Practice Template

Choose a podcast, lecture, or news broadcast.

Round 1: As you listen, write down as many words as you can. Check the spelling and meanings of words you are not sure of.

Round 2: Repeat the process.

Frequency is important. If possible, do this exercise every day. Investing ten to twenty minutes a day on this exercise will pay handsome dividends over time.

Shadowing

Many language learners make use of tapes, radio broadcasts, movies, or podcasts to improve their listening skills. This is good. But, they can get more out of the experience if they go beyond passive listening.

Listening itself can be a pleasant experience, but unless your mind is truly focused on it, the benefits are going to be small.

Some people watch television for years, but they do not necessarily always become smarter or better communicators.

The better way to benefit from radio, podcasts, movies, and other audio and video content for the purpose of improving your communication skills is to do some shadowing.

If you are a beginning English language learner, you can use sites such
Voice of America (VOA) English Learner where the podcasts are at a relatively slow speed.

What you do is follow the speaker, by repeating the phrases they say. Rather than repeating word for word, it's better to follow phrase by phrase.

When you are listening to material that is at normal pace, you can still follow phrase by phrase but because of the speed, you are likely to fall behind.

When that happens, don't worry. Simply continue from another part.
Some people get frustrated with shadowing because they think they should be able to repeat every single word, and that is certainly not necessary.

Idioms

By now, you know a lot of words. But, occasionally you will find that even though you are fully familiar with some words, you cannot figure out what they mean in a sentence. Welcome to the wacky world of idioms; an idiom is "an expression that cannot be understood from the meanings of its separate words but that has a separate meaning of its own" (Learners Dictionary).

Let's say, you are talking to a colleague and she says, "On my job these days, I am carrying the load of work." The idiom, "carry the load" means to be responsible for most of the work. It does not mean actually carrying something on your head head or shoulder. Your own language no doubt has many such metaphors and figures of speech.

If you routinely listen to broadcasts in English or read English magazines or books, you will quickly find that without a good knowledge of a large number of idioms, your understanding will be incomplete.

There are exercises on idioms in this text, but it should only to be a start. As you read, whenever you come across an expression that you cannot readily understand, it may be an idiom. Doublecheck the meaning.

Also, there are many websites and books devoted exclusively to idioms. Spend some time on the subject of idioms and expand the range of idioms you know and understand.

STEP 4
The Road to Reading Riches

In Japan, I have had occasion to ask hundreds of English learners if they ever read books in English. Nine times out of ten, the answer is NO! Some are very honest and say that they do not like reading. Some love reading, but not English books.

I've come to believe that some also do not like to read in English because, even though they can read, they cannot do so fluently. Reading in English, therefore, becomes a chore or something to dread.

Those who do not form the habit of reading in English miss probably the most important opportunity they have to build up their English skills.

Lack of fluency in reading English can be fixed through phonics reading practice. And those who are really determined to improve their English but lack a large vocabulary can begin to build their vocabulary by taking a step back, starting their reading program with graded readers, and gradually working their way up towards regular books and articles for adults.

Those who study textbook after textbook year after year may learn to speak English, but they are frequently surprised when they come across new English expressions that they never learned in their textbooks! They learn a little too late that if they had taken the reading road they would have been much richer in vocabulary, idiomatic expressions, and the use of English that sounds much more natural to the native ear.

Let's Read

As you read an article or book, pay attention not only to new words, but also phrases, and idiomatic expressions. Note down new words you encounter, confirm their meanings through the use of dictionary, and make it a habit to find at least two synonyms and two antonyms for each new word you find. Also, find sample sentences from either the dictionary or from newspapers, magazines, or books.

Use the Dictionary

You will find that the dictionary sometimes gives two, three, or even four or more meanings of a word. It is a good idea to linger over the pages of the dictionary to explore all the different meanings of a word.

Let's say I am reading an article and I come across the word "entice." I go to the Merriam-Webster Dictionary to find its meaning.

I learn from Merriam-Webster that entice is a transitive verbs that means "to attract artfully or **adroitly** or by arousing hope or desire" and that its synonym is "tempt."

If this meaning is still not so clear to me, MerriamWebster offers me two links that can make my life easier:

See entice defined for English-language learners

See entice defined for kids

When I click on the first link, I get the following definition:
"to attract (someone) especially by offering or showing something that is appealing, interesting, etc."

When I click on the link for the word in the kids dictionary, it says:
"to attract by arousing hope or desire"

Meanwhile, I notice a word that I was not familiar with before, "adroitly." I write it down in my vocabulary notebook and search for its meaning, synonyms, and antonyms.

Pronunciation

Some online dictionaries such as MerriamWebster and its associated dictionaries include audio links for those who want to confirm the pronunciation of a word. Please make active use of this because it will help you build more familiarity with the words you encounter.

Use the Thesaurus

MerriamWebster also has a thesaurus feature that gives you both synonyms and antonyms. When you learn about words that are in the same family or share a similar meaning, you increase your chances of being a more versatile communicator because then, you have a wider range of words to choose from. And that allows you to express yourself more clearly.

When I click on the Thesaurus feature I get the following synonyms for entice:

allure, bait, beguile, betray, decoy, lure, lead on, seduce, solicit, tempt

While these words are synonyms, that does not mean that they are always interchangeable. It's a good idea then to expand my research and learn more about each of the words so that I can know exactly when I can use them.

I also get a list of Related Words, as follows:

draw in, inveigle, persuade, rope (in), snow; catch, enmesh (also inmesh), ensnare, entrap, mesh, snare, tangle, trap; bewitch, captivate, charm, enchant, fascinate, magnetize, wile

Near antonyms listed include the following:

alert, caution, forewarn, ward (off), warn; drive (away or off), repulse, turn away

If we linger over these words and review them, when we meet them again, they will not be total strangers to us. The MerriamWebster dictionary also offers examples of how "entice" can be used in a sentence:

Every commercial seemed to be for some tempting snack specifically designed to entice me from my diet.

I have used Merriam Webster as an example, but there are other great dictionaries that you can use, such as the following:

Collins English Dictionary, Macmillan English Dictionary, Longman Dictionary of Contemporary English, The Oxford English Dictionary, Oxford American Dictionary, Oxford Advanced Learners Dictionary

STEP 5
Verbs - #1

Verbs are important in that they play a part in describing actions, events, states, or changes. You put yourself at a considerable disadvantage if you do not know the meanings of verbs you encoounter.

a. Hedges *line* the boulevard.
b. The boulevard *is lined* by hedges.
c. The volcano *erupted* last night.
d. It *snows* a lot in my hometown.
e. She *developed* a new prototype.
f. You *entertained* the crowd well.

If you know the meanings of the verbs you encounter, your life would be that much easier. You do not have to guess. So, expanding your knowledge of verbs is crucial. Rather than just knowing the meanings of verbs, you make them a part of your active vocabulary if you make an effort to use them in sentences, both for in-class practice and in everyday conversation.

Make a sententence with each of the following verbs:

1. become   _____

_____

2. occupy   _____

_____

3. set _____

_____

4. close _____

_____

5. open _____

_____

6. gather _____

_____

7. hold _____

_____

8. stack _____

_____

9. dress _____

_____

10. ready _____

_____

11. load   _____

_____

12. nod   _____

_____

13. show   _____

_____

14. bloom   _____

_____

15. tackle   _____

_____

16. flatten   _____

_____

17. chase   _____

_____

18. feed   _____

_____

19. exchange _____

_____

20. squash _____

_____

21. get over _____

_____

22. kneel _____

_____

23. lend _____

_____

24. sympathize_____

_____

25. vary _____

_____

26. command _____

_____

STEP 6
Homonyms - #1

Homonyms are words that have the same spelling or pronunciation but carry different meanings.

To become a good communicator, you should get to know homonyms intimately, and that means knowing not just the sounds but also the meanings so that you can identify when they are not being used in the proper context.

Use the following pairs of words in sentences to cement your understanding by making a separate sentence for each word.

1. allowed _____

   _____

   aloud _____

   _____

2. bare _____

   _____

   bear _____

   _____

3. break _____

   brake _____

4. caught _____

   court _____

5. dear _____

   deer _____

6. hole _____

   whole _____

7. know _____

_____

   no _____

_____

8. lessen _____

_____

   lesson _____

_____

9. meat _____

_____

   meet _____

_____

10. patience _____

_____

   patients _____

_____

11. passed _____ - _____

_____

past _____

_____

12. peace_____

_____

piece_____

_____

13. plain _____

_____

plane _____

_____

14. road _____

_____

rode_____

_____

15. right _____

_____

write _____

_____

16. rose: _____

_____

rows _____

_____

17. some _____

_____

sum _____

_____

18. tail _____

_____

tale _____

_____

19. threw _____

_____

through _____

_____

20. by _____

_____

buy _____

_____

21. maize _____

_____

maze _____

_____

22. manner _____

_____

manor _____

_____

23. missed _____

_____

mist _____

_____

24. morning _____

_____

mourning _____

_____

25. knot _____

_____

not _____

_____

26. peak _____

_____

peek _____

_____

27. pedal_____

_____

peddle_____

_____

28. poll_____

_____

pole_____

_____

29. pray_____

_____

prey_____

_____

30. presence_____

_____

presents_____

_____

31. reign_____

_____

rain_____

_____

32. for_____

_____

fore_____

_____

four_____

_____

33. feat_____

_____

feet_____

_____

34. grown _____

_____

groan _____

_____

35. guessed _____

_____

guest _____

_____

36. gym _____

_____

Jim _____

_____

37. hairy _____

_____

Harry _____

_____

37. heel _____

_____

heal _____

_____

38. sale _____

_____

sell _____

_____

39. seam _____

_____

seem _____

_____

40. slay _____

_____

sleigh _____

_____

41. soar_____

_____

sore_____

_____

42. maize_____

_____

maze_____

_____

43. altar_____

_____

alter_____

_____

44. appraise_____

_____

apprise_____

_____

45. overdo_____

_____

overdue_____

_____

46. amoral_____

_____

immoral_____

_____

47. balmy_____

_____

barmy_____

_____

48. bazaar_____

_____

bizarre_____

_____

STEP 7

Verb Tenses - #1

Mistakes with verb tenses are some of the most common errors English learners make.

Let's review:

Simple Present	Simple Past	Simple Future
live	*lived*	*will live*
Present Continuous	Past Continuous	Future Continuous
am living	*was living*	*will be living*
Present Perfect	Past Perfect	Future Perfect
have lived	*had lived*	*will have lived*
Present Perfect Continuous	Past Perfect Continuous	Future Perfect Continuous
have been living	*had been living*	*will have been living*

How about trying your hand at conjugating a few verbs?

Verb Conjugation

Work

Simple Present	Simple Past	Simple Future
Present Continuous	Past Continuous	Future Continuous
Present Perfect	Past Perfect	Future Perfect
Present Perfect Continuous	Past Perfect Continuous	Future Perfect Continuous

Seek

Simple Present	Simple Past	Simple Future
Present Continuous	Past Continuous	Future Continuous
Present Perfect	Past Perfect	Future Perfect
Present Perfect Continuous	Past Perfect Continuous	Future Perfect Continuous

Buy

Simple Present	Simple Past	Simple Future
Present Continuous	Past Continuous	Future Continuous
Present Perfect	Past Perfect	Future Perfect
Present Perfect Continuous	Past Perfect Continuous	Future Perfect Continuous

Complete the following table. Check the meanings of words you do not know.

Verb Tenses			
No.	Verb	Past tense	Past Participle
1	Abide		
2	Alight		
3	Arise		
4	Awake		
5	Backbite		
6	Backfit		
7	Backlight		
8	Backslide		
9	Be		
10	Bear		
11	Beat		
12	Become		
13	Befall		
14	Bend		

Verb Tenses			
No.	Verb	Past tense	Past Participle
15	Bereave		
16	Beseech		
17	Break		
18	Bottlefeed		
19	Beset		
20	Bespeak		
21	Bestrew		
22	Bestride		
23	Bet		
24	Betake		
25	Bethink		
26	Beweep		
27	Blow		
28	Breastfeed		
29	Breed		

No.	Verb	Past tense	Past Participle
30	Bid		
31	Bide		
32	Bind		
33	Bite		
34	Bleed		
35	Blend		
36	Bless		
37	Bust		
38	Buy		
39	Burst		
40	Cast		
41	Burn		
42	Bring		
43	Broadcast		
44	Browbeat		

Verb Tenses

No.	Verb	Past tense	Past Participle
45	Build		
46	Clothe		
47	Come		
48	Cost		
49	Cowrite		
50	Crash-dive		
51	Creep		
52	Crossbreed		
53	Crow		
54	Cut		
55	Dare		
56	Daydream		
57	Deal		
58	Disprove		
59	Engrave		

Verb Tenses

No.	Verb	Past tense	Past Participle
60	Fall		
61	Feed		
62	Feel		
63	Fight		
64	Find		
65	Fit		
66	Flee		
67	Fling		
68	Fly		
69	Forbear		
70	Forbid		
71	Force-feed		
72	Forecast		
73	Forgo		
74	Drill		

Verb Tenses

No.	Verb	Past tense	Past Participle
75	Foresee		
76	Foreshadow		
77	Foretell		
78	Forget		
79	Forgive		
80	Forsake		
81	Forswear		
82	Gild		
83	Gird		
84	Give		
85	Gnaw		
86	Go		
87	Grind		
88	Grow		
89	Grift		

Verb Tenses			
No.	Verb	Past tense	Past Participle
90	Hand-feed		
91	Hang (on the wall)		
92	Hang (someone)		
93	Have		
94	Hear		
95	Heave		
96	Hew		
97	Hit		
98	Hoist		
99	Hold		
100	House-sit		
101	Hurt		
102	Inlay		
103	Input		
104	Interest		

Verb Tenses			
No.	Verb	Past tense	Past Participle
105	Interweave		
106	Keep		
107	Freeze		
108	Gainsay		
109	Get		
110	Ghostwrite		
111	Kneel		
112	Knit		
113	Know		
114	Lay		
115	Lead		
116	Leap		
117	Leave		
118	Leaven		
1119	Lend		

STEP 8
Quick Response Practice

Knowing how to answer particular types of questions can be useful to you in all areas of your life as a communicator. Give short answers to the following questions to gauge how readily you are able to answer questions in English.

1) Where do you like to go for holidays?

2) How often do you visit your hometown?

3) What time do you usually get up?

4) Where does your best friend work?

5) When was the last time you talked to your boss?

6) How many people live in your home?

7) What kind of business are you in?

8) When was the last time you visited a zoo?

9) Where would you suggest I go for a quick lunch?

10) What's your favorite mode of transportation?

11) How much free time do you usually have each week?

12) On average, how much sleep do you get each day?

13) What's your dream job?

14) What's your experience been with online shopping?

15) What's the last book you read?

STEP 9
Word Forms #1: Verbs, Nouns, Adjectives

Knowing the correct forms of words is essential for effective communication. Whether you are writing reports or participating in a meeting or negotiation, being able to use the correct forms of words can help you express yourself in ways that signal professionalism and attention to detail.

Here is your opportunity to review some verbs and their nouns and adjectives.

Identify the nouns and adjectives for the verbs indicated and form sentences using each form of the word.

1.

VERB	Compare	
NOUN		
ADJECTIVE		

2.

VERB		
NOUN		
ADJECTIVE		

3.

VERB	Market	
NOUN		
ADJECTIVE		

4.

VERB	Consume	
NOUN		
ADJECTIVE		

5.

VERB	Compete	
NOUN		
ADJECTIVE		

6.

VERB	Attract	
NOUN		
ADJECTIVE		

7.

VERB	Inspire	
NOUN		
ADJECTIVE		

8.

VERB	Specify	
NOUN		
ADJECTIVE		

9.

VERB	Resolve	
NOUN		
ADJECTIVE		

10.

VERB	Provide	
NOUN		
ADJECTIVE		

11.

VERB	Obligate	
NOUN		
ADJECTIVE		

12.

VERB	Determine	
NOUN		
ADJECTIVE		

13

VERB	Demonstrate	
NOUN		
ADJECTIVE		

14.

VERB	Abhor	
NOUN		
ADJECTIVE		

15.

VERB	Strategize	
NOUN		
ADJECTIVE		

16.

VERB	Substitute	
NOUN		
ADJECTIVE		

17.

VERB	Counterfeit	
NOUN		
ADJECTIVE		

18.

VERB	Remunerate	
NOUN		
ADJECTIVE		

19.

VERB	Abrade	
NOUN		
ADJECTIVE		

20.

VERB	Knot	
NOUN		
ADJECTIVE		

21.

VERB	Abase	
NOUN		
ADJECTIVE		

22.

VERB	Repel	
NOUN		
ADJECTIVE		

STEP 10

Homonyms - #2

Make sentences with each pair of words to demonstrate your understanding of the meanings of the two words.

1. banned_____

   _____

   band_____

   _____

2. dye_____

   _____

   die_____

   _____

3. fair_____

   _____

   fare_____

   _____

4. flower_____

_____

flour_____

_____

5. hear_____

_____

here_____

_____

6. hire_____

_____

higher_____

_____

7. hour_____

_____

our_____

_____

8. I_____

    _____

    eye_____

    _____

9. jeans_____

    _____

    genes_____

    _____

10. maid_____

    _____

    made_____

    _____

11. cell_____

    _____

    sell_____

    _____

12. pale _____

_____

pail _____

_____

13. principal _____

_____

principle _____

_____

14. reflex _____

_____

reflects _____

_____

15. sail _____

_____

sale _____

_____

16. sea_____

_____

see_____

_____

17. scene_____

_____

seen_____

_____

18. sense_____

_____

cents_____

_____

19. sew_____

_____

so_____

_____

20. son_____

_____

sun_____

_____

21. soul_____

_____

sole_____

_____

22. meat_____

_____

meet_____

_____

23. affect_____

_____

effect_____

_____

24. aisle_____

_____

I'll_____

_____

26. ant_____

_____

aunt_____

_____

27. ate_____

_____

eight_____

_____

28. bald_____

_____

bawled_____

_____

29. bare_____

_____

bear_____

_____

30. billed_____

_____

built_____

_____

31. chili_____

_____

chilly_____

_____

32. close_____

_____

clothes_____

_____

STEP 11

Word Forms - #2: (Verbs, Nouns, Adjectives)

Find the noun and the adjective for each word. Then, make sentences for each.

1.

		SAMPLE SENTENCE / MY SENTENCE
VERB	Require	
NOUN		
ADJECTIVE		

2.

		SAMPLE SENTENCE / MY SENTENCE
VERB	Protect	
NOUN		
ADJECTIVE		

3.

		SAMPLE SENTENCE / MY SENTENCE
VERB	Imply	
NOUN		
ADJECTIVE		

4.

	SAMPLE SENTENCE / MY SENTENCE
VERB Consider	
NOUN	
ADJECTIVE	

5.

	SAMPLE SENTENCE / MY SENTENCE
VERB Categorize	
NOUN	
ADJECTIVE	

6.

	SAMPLE SENTENCE / MY SENTENCE
VERB Develop	
NOUN	
ADJECTIVE	

7.

	SAMPLE SENTENCE / MY SENTENCE
VERB	Strengthen	
NOUN		
ADJECTIVE		

8.

	SAMPLE SENTENCE / MY SENTENCE
VERB	Substitute	
NOUN		
ADJECTIVE		

9.

	SAMPLE SENTENCE / MY SENTENCE
VERB	Select	
NOUN		
ADJECTIVE		

10.

	SAMPLE SENTENCE / MY SENTENCE
VERB	Attend	
NOUN		
ADJECTIVE		

11.

	SAMPLE SENTENCE / MY SENTENCE
VERB	Arrange	
NOUN		
ADJECTIVE		

12.

	SAMPLE SENTENCE / MY SENTENCE
VERB	Register	
NOUN		
ADJECTIVE		

13.

	SAMPLE SENTENCE / MY SENTENCE
VERB — Evaluate	
NOUN	
ADJECTIVE	

14.

	SAMPLE SENTENCE / MY SENTENCE
VERB — Reserve	
NOUN	
ADJECTIVE	

15.

	SAMPLE SENTENCE / MY SENTENCE
VERB — Preserve	
NOUN	
ADJECTIVE	

16.

	SAMPLE SENTENCE / MY SENTENCE
VERB	Initiate	
NOUN		
ADJECTIVE		

17.

	SAMPLE SENTENCE / MY SENTENCE
VERB	Recur	
NOUN		
ADJECTIVE		

18.

	SAMPLE SENTENCE / MY SENTENCE
VERB	Rely	
NOUN		
ADJECTIVE		

19.

		SAMPLE SENTENCE / MY SENTENCE
VERB	Reduce	
NOUN		
ADJECTIVE		

20.

		SAMPLE SENTENCE / MY SENTENCE
VERB	Observe	
NOUN		
ADJECTIVE		

21.

		SAMPLE SENTENCE / MY SENTENCE
VERB	Warn	
NOUN		
ADJECTIVE		

22.

		SAMPLE SENTENCE / MY SENTENCE
VERB	Innovate	
NOUN		
ADJECTIVE		

23.

		SAMPLE SENTENCE / MY SENTENCE
VERB	Fail	
NOUN		
ADJECTIVE		

24.

		SAMPLE SENTENCE / MY SENTENCE
VERB	Duplicate	
NOUN		
ADJECTIVE		

25.

	SAMPLE SENTENCE / MY SENTENCE
VERB — Allocate	
NOUN	
ADJECTIVE	

26.

	SAMPLE SENTENCE / MY SENTENCE
VERB — Access	
NOUN	
ADJECTIVE	

27.

	SAMPLE SENTENCE / MY SENTENCE
VERB — Restrain	
NOUN	
ADJECTIVE	

28.

	SAMPLE SENTENCE / MY SENTENCE
VERB	Conserve
NOUN	
ADJECTIVE	

29.

	SAMPLE SENTENCE / MY SENTENCE
VERB	Interrupt
NOUN	
ADJECTIVE	

30.

	SAMPLE SENTENCE / MY SENTENCE
VERB	Intervene
NOUN	
ADJECTIVE	

31.

		SAMPLE SENTENCE / MY SENTENCE
VERB	Intercept	
NOUN		
ADJECTIVE		

32.

		SAMPLE SENTENCE / MY SENTENCE
VERB	Submit	
NOUN		
ADJECTIVE		

33.

		SAMPLE SENTENCE / MY SENTENCE
VERB	Estimate	
NOUN		
ADJECTIVE		

34.

	SAMPLE SENTENCE / MY SENTENCE
VERB Quarrel	
NOUN	
ADJECTIVE	

35.

	SAMPLE SENTENCE / MY SENTENCE
VERB Situate	
NOUN	
ADJECTIVE	

36.

	SAMPLE SENTENCE / MY SENTENCE
VERB Entitle	
NOUN	
ADJECTIVE	

37.

		SAMPLE SENTENCE / MY SENTENCE
VERB	Impose	
NOUN		
ADJECTIVE		

38.

		SAMPLE SENTENCE / MY SENTENCE
VERB	Politicize	
NOUN		
ADJECTIVE		

39.

		SAMPLE SENTENCE / MY SENTENCE
VERB	Adopt	
NOUN		
ADJECTIVE		

STEP 12
Verbs - #2

Make sentences with each of the following verbs.

1. take

2. interview

3. repair

4. take off

5. dock

6. activate

7. insert

8. pass

9. turn

10. regulate

11. use

12. crack

13. tear

14. yell

15. hail

16. twist

17. stand

18. sit

19. park

20. call

21. collate

22. prepare

23. break

24. shutter

25. pursue

26. pick

27. draw

28. ascend

29. cage

30. secure

31. batten

32. corral

33. chop

34. scream

35. approach

36. blanket

37. fasten

38. roar

39. pluck

40. seal

41. slam

42. hoard

43. attend

44. hide

45. divide

46. misread

47. mean

48. melt

49. misspell

50. misunderstand

51. nose-dive

52. ensure

STEP 13
Know Your Prepositions

Prepositions usually show relationships between or among things or people. You might have a book **on** a table, see someone standing **next to** a tree, or spy a cat **under** a desk. Here are some common prepositons.

List of Prepositions / Preposition Phrases

about	beside	near	under
above	besides	of	until
across	between	off	up
after	beyond	on	upon
against	by	out	with
along	despite	over	within
among	down	since	without
around	during	through	in between
at	for	throughout	in front of
before	from	till	next to
behind	in	to	on top of
below	into	toward	out of
beneath	like	towards	back to

Some prepositions are more troublesome than others.

Subject	Verb		Object
The little children	played	in	the garden.
	in		*(preposition)*
	the garden		*(object of the preposition)*
	in the garden		*prepositional phrase*

The team went to the park in the evening.

	to the park	*prepositional phrase*
	in the evening	*prepositional phrase*

"Place" (to the park) usually comes before "Time" (in the evening).

Meanwhile, it is important to understand the following three prepositions of place:

At

a) used to talk about something in a particular place or area, for example, park, airport, school, concert, stadium, etc.

>She was **at the park** when the hot air balloon came down.
>We stayed overnight **at the train station.**
>We all gathered **at home**.
>I have nothing to do **at work today**.

b) used to point to an address

>He lives **at** 14 Rolland Lane, Sussex.
>They live **at** Hyde Park Mansions.

c) used to talk about public places or institutions

>We met **at** the airport five years ago.
>We went to study **at** the university library.
>The festival started **at** the station.

d) used to refer to organized social events

> It was wonderful to see all my friends **at the rave party.**
> The professor spoke passionately **at the conference.**
> Everyone was **at the meeting** this morning.

e) used to talk about a place on a journey

> I want to stop **at Ikebukuro Station.**

f) used to talk about parts of a place
> They are working **at** the back of the house.
> **At** the front of the house, you will see nothng but flowers.
> There is an antenna **at** the top of the house.
> There is a message **at** the back of the tome.

In

a) used to talk about something in an enclosed place or space, for example, room, office, tent, building, etc.

> We were **in** the classroom when the rain started.
> All the fun is **in** the kitchen.
> The water **in** the washroon is running.

b) used to talk about a road or street

> We saw him **in** Princeton Road.
> The stores **in** that street are just fabulous.
> He lost his hat **in** the street.

c) used to talk about a village, town, city or any large space

> We are going to be **in** Tokyo tonight.
> Life **in** a village is quiet and peaceful.
> Call me when you are **in** the area.
> We lived **in** Shanghai many years ago.
> There are so many ducks frolicking **in** the park.

d) used to talk about a country or geographical area
> We are **in** Denmark for a photo shoot.
> We got these mushrooms **in** the hills.
> That guy lives **in** the mountains.
> These shells can be found **in** the river.

Use each of the following prepositions/prepositional phrases to make a sentence:

1. in a car

2. through the tunnel

3. on a bullet train

4. above

5. under

6. across

7. around

8. on top of

9. in front of

10. below

11. beneath

12. far from

13. near

14. over

15. to the right of

16. to the left of

17. next to

18. beside

19. between

20. in back of

21. by bus

22. close to

23. inside

24. outside

25. underneath

26. within

27. against

28. along

29. through

30. down

31. outside of

32. by train

33. by plane

34. by ferry

35. on a bullet train

36. in an air-conditioned coach

37. on a jumbo jet

38. into the train

39. out of the bus

40. off the train

41. onto the truck

STEP 14
Preposition Combinations

Some prepositions combine with verbs, adjectives or nouns. For example, the expression "interested in" is a preposition combination. This particular combination requires you to use a gerund (-ing form acting as a noun - reading, sleeping, eating, etc.) after the preposition. Thus,

I am interested in read.	WRONG
I am interested to read.	WRONG
I am interested in *reading*.	CORRECT

The word "reading" after the preposition is referred to as the object of the preposition.

There are a number of preposition combinations besides "interested in" that require you to use a gerund as the object of the prepositon. Here are some examples:

The typhoon **kept us** *waiting* in the hotel for hours.
I am **looking forward to** *hearing* from you.
My parents are **excited about** *visiting* Tasmania.
I **thought about** *writing* an essay.

Noun + Preposition	Adjective + Preposition	Verb + Preposition
a solution to	amazed at	depend on
a lack of	shocked by	rely on
an expert at	worried about	believe in
influence on	proud of	deal with
evidence of	different from	fight against
possibility of	related to	contribute to

Make sentences to demonstrate your understanding of the following preposition combinations.

1. stop someone from

2. prevent someone from

3. believe in

4. build on

5. participate in

6. keep someone from

7. succeed in

8. thank someone for

9. be accused of

10. be responsible for

11. be capable of

12. have a reason for

13. be guilty of

14. have an excuse for

15. instead of

16. forgive someone for

17. take advantage of

18. blame someone for

19. take care of

20. talk of

21. be tired of

22. apologize for

23. insist on

24. think about

25. in addition to

26. talk about

27. be committed to

28. dream about

29. be devoted to

30. complain about

31. be worried about

32. be excited about

33. be used to

34. complain of

35. think of

36. dream of

37. wind up

38. resort to

39. end up

40. consign to

41. dispose of

42. sift through

43. pile on

STEP 15

Common Occupations

In your everyday interactions, you might have to deal with people from different occupational backgrounds. If you are not sure about the meaning, take some time to find out. Here are a few.

Make a sentence with each of of the listed occupations to demonstrate your understanding of the meaning.

1. Retail salesperson

2. Flight attendant

3. Pilot

4. Cashier

5. Housekeeper

6. Office clerk

7. Janitor

English Language Mastermind - Everett Ofori

8. Psychologist

9. Bookkeeper

10. Neuroscientist

11. Orderly

12. Secretary

13. Security guard

14. Landscaping worker

15. Travel agent

16. Dermatologist

17. Internist

18. Gynecologist

19. Psychiatrist

20. Veterinarian

21. Obstetrician

22. Pediatrician

23. Ophthalmologist

24. Orthopedist

25. Cardiologist

26. Neurologist

27. Rental clerk

28. Personnel director

29. Bill collector

30. Anesthesiologist

31. Sales representative

32. Novelist

33. Preschool teacher

34. Reporter

35. Machinist

36. Sign painter

37. Computer programmer

38. Pharmacist

39. Police officer

40. Postal mail carrier

41. Movie extra

42. Welder

43. Dental assistant

44. Surgeon

45. Firefighter

46. Chaplain

47. Social worker

48. Chief executive

49. Administrative support worker

50. Civil engineer

51. Mechanical engineer

52. Public relations specialist

53. Hotel desk clerk

54. Sculptor

55. Interviewer

56. Industrial engineer

57. Brew master

58. Bank teller

59. Sommelier

60. Provost

61. Dean

62. Deacon

STEP 16

By versus Until

Have you been in a situation where you were not sure whether to use by or until in a sentence? Let's explore this together. Here are some common situations in which you see the use of "by."

By 6 o'clock   By tomorrow night   By next month
By Thursday   By Christmas   By next year

In all of these cases, the time, month, period, or season mentioned is seen as a deadline.

The focus is on the deadline, that is, whether something will happen or not happen before or at the deadline.

I will finish dinner by 6 p.m. (Maybe, I will eat at 4 p.m., maybe, at 5:15 p.m., but by 5:59 p.m., I should definitely be ready to put down my fork, having already completed the meal.

Likewise, if we say that the doctor will come in by 10 a.m., it means that the doctor might show up at 8 a.m. or maybe, 9:10 a.m., but certainly, before the clock strikes 10, she should have come in!

Now, consider this:

I should complete the program by the end of the year.

It seems that when December 31st rolls around and you ask me about the program, I should very likely be able to say that I am done.

Until

The word until, which is often shortened to till in spoken English, focuses on what happens from one instance of time and continues to another instance of time.

In this case, the focus is on something that starts at A and continues to the point or time of B.

The party will go from 7 p.m. (A) until 11 p.m. (B).

By and Until in the Same Type of Sentence: Check the Meaning

You need to be home until 12 noon. (This means you are already home, and you need to stay at home from the moment you get this message right up to 12 noon.

You need to be home by 12 noon.

(This means you are not at home. But, you must get home some time before 12 noon.

Exercise

1. Don't do anything *until* / *by* I return.

2. I am not feeling well. I will stay in bed *until* / *by* morning.

3. We are going to play a game. Don't open this box *until* / *by* I come back.

4. This bill needs to be paid *until* / *by* December 1st.

5. We had a tough negotiation, which continued *until* / *by* the crack of dawn.

6. The assignment is due *until* / *by* tomorrow morning.

7. The kids need to get home *until* / *by* 9 p.m.

8. We lived in an apartment *until* / *by* last year.

9. Details about the contract will not be available *until* / *by* the summer.

10. I will have finished sewing the dress *until* / *by* 5 o'clock tonight.

STEP 17
Word Forms - #3
Nouns & Their Verbs

The Cambridge dictionary defines a noun as a "word that refers to a person, place, thing, event, substance, or quality." Some nouns are countable (e.g., pen, pens; table, tables; application, applications). Others are uncountable (safety, money, rice).

Nouns

A person:	girl, engineer, friend, neighbor
A thing:	cat, apartment, tree, city
An idea, quality, or state:	honor, freedom, sadness, birth

We can also consider nouns from the following perspectives:

Common nouns: refer to people or things in general
(village, tunnel, night, happiness)

Proper nouns: identify a particular person, place, or thing
(Sarah, Joseph, Kenji, Friday, Australia)

Concrete nouns: refers to people and things that you can see, touch, hear, smell, or taste
(giraffe, mansion, flower, snow, song)

Abstract nouns: refer to ideas, qualities, or conditions, which are not physical and thus cannot be seen or touched
(humor, time, happiness)

Collective nouns: refer to groups of people or things
(family, committee, team, jury)

In American English, "The committee is having a meeting" will be considered correct. Most collective nouns take the singular form of the verb.

In British English, while the earlier example would be correct, it would also be correct to say or write, "The committee are having a meeting."

It is important to understand that it is possible for a noun to belong to several different categories. For example, sadness is a common noun. Sadness is also an abstract noun. As well, Mount Kilmanjaro is a concrete noun. It is also a proper noun.[1]

Some nouns are more than one word. We call these compound nouns, and not surprisingly, a compound noun contains at least one noun.

They come in three main forms:

Closed form	**Hyphenated form**	**Open form**
keyboard	son-in-law	swimming pool
toothpaste	six-pack	full moon
makeup	seven-year-old	steak house
overthrow	check-in	happy hour
redhead		sandwich bar
blackboard		gift shop
		tea room
		money transfer
		middle class

---

[1] *Oxford Dictionaries* http://en.oxforddictionaries.com

Nouns: Common Endings

It is useful to be able to identify nouns since that can affect how they are used in a sentence.

Here are some common noun endings and their corresponding examples:

Ending	Noun examples
-ance	alliance, endurance, appearance, clearance, guidance, acceptance, ignorance, attendance, grievance, dominance, disturbace, assistance, appliance, maintenance, distance, insurance, allowance, instance, substance, distance, importance, resemblance
-ancy	inconstancy, buoyancy, hesitancy, discrepancy, redundancy, militancy, occupancy, pregnancy, accountancy, buoyancy, infancy, expectancy, tenancy, consultancy, ascendancy, truancy
-ence	reverence, adherence, coherence, consequence, confidence, absence, patience, convenience, experience, preference, conference, silence, existence, sequence, coincidence, sentence, insistence, affluence, evidence, essence, reference, audience, recurrence, difference, innocence, presence, influence
-ency	constituency, proficiency, transparency, leniency, urgency, efficiency, consistency, tendency, frequency, decency, sufficiency, fluency, currency, agency
-tion	addition, duration, nation, solution, ambition, edition, caution, donation, vacation, accommodation, location, creation, rotation, education, mediation, action, connection, reception, affection, interruption, description, collection, infection, deception
-sion	immersion, comprehension, aversion, conversion, apprehension, diversion, extension, version, permission, discussion, commission, expression, aggression, admission, succession, impression, emission

Now, you know the nouns. Do you know their corresponding verbs?

1.

		Make sentences to demonstrate your understanding of the difference in usage
Noun	Application	
Verb		

2.

		Make sentences to demonstrate your understanding of the difference in usage
Noun	Theory	
Verb		

3.

		Make sentences to demonstrate your understanding of the difference in usage
Noun	Competition	
Verb		

4.

		Make sentences to demonstrate your understanding of the difference in usage
Noun	Repetition	
Verb		

5.

		Make sentences to demonstrate your understanding of the difference in usage
Noun	Criticism	
Verb		

6.

		Make sentences to demonstrate your understanding of the difference in usage
Noun	Prosperity	
Verb		

7.

		Make sentences to demonstrate your understanding of the difference in usage
Noun	Decision	
Verb		

8.

		Make sentences to demonstrate your understanding of the difference in usage
Noun	Production	
Verb		

9.

		Make sentences to demonstrate your understanding of the difference in usage
Noun	Economy	
Verb		

10.

		Make sentences to demonstrate your understanding of the difference in usage
Noun	Negotiation	
Verb		

11.

	Make sentences to demonstrate your understanding of the difference in usage
Noun Finale	
Verb	

12.

	Make sentences to demonstrate your understanding of the difference in usage
Noun Nation	
Verb	

13.

	Make sentences to demonstrate your understanding of the difference in usage
Noun Interpretation	
Verb	

14.

	Make sentences to demonstrate your understanding of the difference in usage
Noun Maintenance	
Verb	

15.

	Make sentences to demonstrate your understanding of the difference in usage
Noun Mechanism	
Verb	

STEP 18
Verbs followed by Gerunds

Earlier on, we talked about nouns. There is a class of verbs that behave like nouns. These are called gerunds, and end in "-ing". Since gerunds function as NOUNS, this means that they can be the subject or object of a sentence and behave in other ways that nouns do.

Here are some examples:
>**Hiking** is what she loves to do.
>Kim goes **swimming** once a week.

Verbs followed by Gerunds

Here is a question for you. What do you enjoy doing? You might say,
>I enjoy **swimming**.

The word swimming in the sentence above is an example of a gerund. Some verbs require you to use gerunds. One of those verbs, of course, is enjoy.

Advise

If there is no noun or pronoun object after "advise," use a gerund. Otherwise, use the infinitive (to + verb).
>*My teacher advised purchasing a chemistry set.*
>*My teacher advised me to purchase a chemistry set.*

It is true that a verb such as "suggest" can be followed by "ing" but of course it does not mean that this is the only pattern. There could be other patterns depending on what you are trying to say:
>I suggest taking a train.
>I suggest that you take a train.
>I suggest you take a train.

Exercise: Use a gerund after each of the following verbs to form a sentence.

1. miss

2. enjoy

3. fancy

4. appreciate

5. discuss

6. finish

7. dislike

8. suggest

9. delay

10. postpone (put off)

11. involve

12. mind

13. risk

14. quit

15. keep

16. mention

17. consider

18. keep on

19. practice

20. recall

21. anticipate

22. complete

23. understand

24. tolerate

25. imagine

26. deny

27. admit

28. celebrate

29. detest

30. discontinue

31. dispute

32. endure

33. escape

34. explain

35. feel like

36. give up

37. justify

38. mention

39. postpone

40. prohibit

41. recall

42. resist

STEP 19

Go, Play, or Do?

What are your hobbies? Do you like going biking? Do you like doing judo? Do you like playing handball?

It can at times be confusing what verb goes with what activity.

Go

These usually involve activities that end in -ing (fishing, hiking, kayaking). These activities usually require a person to go somewhere in order to engage in the activity.

Play

These usually involve ball sports or competitive activities. An exception is "playing a musical instrument" which does not involve a ball and is not necessarily competitive. There are many exceptions in English, which is why you should not rely only on rules to improve your English. When you read extensively, you get the chance to see both the rules and the exceptions at play.

Do

These usually involve recreational activities where no ball is involved.
Also, they may be non-team sports.

See the next page for a handy list. There will be a quiz to see how many of them you can remember.

Go	Play	Do
biking	tennis	judo
bird-watching	soccer	karate
boating	handball	taekwondo
bowling	badminton	sports
camping	chess	fencing
canoeing	squash	boxing
window shopping	volley ball	weight lifting
swimming	rugby	aerobics
snorkelling	baseball	gymnastics
sledding	board games	kung fu
skinny-dipping	snooker	yoga
skiing	cricket	a crossword puzzle
dancing	golf	athletics
mountain climbing	table tennis	window shopping
jogging	a musical instrument	aerobics
hunting	checkers	archery
hiking	games	tai chi
bungee jumping	dead	a crossword puzzle
fishing	possum	exercise

Note: Pay attention to exceptions such as: I do swimming on Saturdays while I do art on Sundays.

English Language Mastermind - Everett Ofori   117

Go, Play, or Do?

Word	Sentence
skating	
athletics	
ballet	
archery	
roller-skating	
tai chi	
riding	
sailing	
gymnastics	
camping	
weight-lifting	
cycling	
ice hockey	
board games	
judo	
volleyball	

STEP 20

Verbs followed by Infinitives

What is an infinitive? It is a combination of "to" and "the simple form of a verb," for example, to eat, to go, to sleep, etc.).

Just as some verbs are followed by gerunds (-ing), others are followed by the infinitive.

Here are some sentences in which the verbs are followed by infinitives:

> I hope *to go* abroad some day.
> I plan *to meet* my friend tomorrow.
> I have *decided to* start a new project next week.

Please form a sentence by following each of the verbs with an infinitive:

1. yearn

2. wish

3. wait

4. vow

5. try

6. threaten

7. tend

8. swear

9. start

10. remember

11. regret

12. refuse

13. pretend

14. prepare

15. neglect

16. appear

17. hesitate

18. hate

19. happen

20. get

21. fail

22. deserve

23. dread

24. would like

25. agree

26. swear

27. crave

28. threaten

29. refuse

30. propose

31. promise

32. pretend

33. prepare

34. plan

35. neglect

36. willing

37. learn

38. intend

STEP 21
Focus on Nouns

Here are some more nouns you need to know. If you are not sure about the meaning of any of these words, please make it a point to find out.

Ending	Noun examples
-cion	suspicion, coercion
-ian	amphibian, egalitarian, humanitarian, authoritarian, mathematician, dietitian, disciplinarian, logician, optician, physician, thespian, vegetarian
-ism	egotism, alcoholism, optimism, plagiarism, Judaism, conservatism, activism, ageism, Americanism, anarchism, Buddhism, colonialism, communism, Darwinism, escapism, expansionism, euphemism, extremism, feminism
-ist	abolitionist, accompanist, acupuncturist, anaesthetist, bicyclist, cellist, fascist, flutist, gemologist, geologist, hair stylist, panelist, pharmacist
-ment	government, development, department, moment, agreement, movement, treatment, statement, investment, equipment, arrangement, settlement, establishment, involvement, excitement, tournament, apartment, encouragement
-ness	faithfulness, coarseness, firmness, attentiveness, indebtedness, brightness, gloominess, awkwardness, forgiveness, promptness, cleanliness, righteousness, abruptness, gratefulness, shyness, cheerfulness, wilderness, darkness, goodness, sickness, smoothness

Make a sentence with each of the following nouns:

1. trend

2. emphasis

3. growth

4. technology

5. sales

6. source

7. customers

8. avenue

9. information

10. association

11. quality

12. announcement

13. habit

14. dispenser

15. comprehension

16. suggestion

17. priority

18. confusion

19. protest

20. environment

21. specialty

22. coverage

23. primer

24. availability

25. improvement

26. judgment

27. maintenance

28. responsibility

29. completion

30. duty

31. assistance

32. calculation

33. circumstance

34. petition

35. identification

36. success

37. succession

38. internship

39. performance

40. attraction

41. shuttle

42. investigation

43. delivery

44. enclosure

45. excursion

46. conversation

47. advertisement

48. turbulence

49. collection

50. foolishness

51. subscription

52. registration

53. submission

54. popularity

55. reception

56. dissatisfaction

57. information

58. promotion

59. loan

60. qualification

61. candidate

62. backwater

63. portion

64. nuance

65. renown

STEP 22
Word Forms - #4: Nouns, Verbs & Adjectives

You have another opportunity here to review your understanding of word forms. Here is an exercise that will help you become more familiar with words and their various forms.

1.

		Make sentences to demonstrate your understanding of the differences in usage
Noun	acceptance	
Verb	accept	
Adjective	acceptable	

2.

		Make sentences to demonstrate your understanding of the differences in usage
Noun	achievement	
Verb	achieve	
Adjective	achievable	

3.

		Make sentences to demonstrate your understanding of the differences in usage
Noun	action/act	
Verb	act	
Adjective	active	

4.

		Make sentences to demonstrate your understanding of the differences in usage
Noun	enforcement	
Verb	enforce	
Adjective	enforced	

5.

		Make sentences to demonstrate your understanding of the differences in usage
Noun	addition	
Verb	add	
Adjective	additional	

6.

		Make sentences to demonstrate your understanding of the differences in usage
Noun	adjustment	
Verb	adjust	
Adjective	adjustable	

7.

		Make sentences to demonstrate your understanding of the differences in usage
Noun	admiration	
Verb	admire	
Adjective	admirable	

8.

		Make sentences to demonstrate your understanding of the differences in usage
Noun	advice	
Verb	advise	
Adjective	advisable	

9.

		Make sentences to demonstrate your understanding of the differences in usage
Noun	mass	
Verb	amass	
Adjective	massive	

10.

		Make sentences to demonstrate your understanding of the differences in usage
Noun	annoyance	
Verb	annoy	
Adjective	annoying	

11.

		Make sentences to demonstrate your understanding of the differences in usage
Noun	approach	
Verb	approach	
Adjective	approachable	

12.

		Make sentences to demonstrate your understanding of the differences in usage
Noun	attention	
Verb	attend	
Adjective	attentive	

13.

		Make sentences to demonstrate your understanding of the differences in usage
Noun	enhancement	
Verb	enhance	
Adjective	enhanced	

14.

		Make sentences to demonstrate your understanding of the differences in usage
Noun	integration	
Verb	integrate	
Adjective	integrated	

STEP 23

Verbs Followed by Gerunds or Infinitives

We covered verbs that are followed by gerunds, for example, enjoy. We also covered verbs that are followed by infinitives, fo example, hope. There are other verbs that can take either a gerund or an infinitive. In some cases, whether a gerund follows the verb or an infinitive does not affect the meaning of the sentence.

In other cases, whether you use a gerund or an infinitive after the verb makes a difference in the meaning of the sentence.

No Change in Meaning

It started to snow right after the party. / It started snowing right after the party.

He began to do his homework as soon as he got home.
He began doing his homework as soon as he got home.

I love to read. / I love reading.

two sentences, one using the gerund and the other using the infinitive.

In some cases, even though there is no change in meaning, the structures vary.

Advise / Allow / Permit / Forbid

I wouldn't advise going to class late. (Not: I wouldn't advise to go to class late.)

For the above, use -ing because the verb 'advise' here has no object. If there is an object, then, you may use the infinitive.

I wouldn't advise **you** to go to class late.

Verb	Gerund sentence	Infinitive sentence
continue		
like		
hate		
can't bear		
can't stand		
cease		
neglect		
prefer		
propose		
advise		
forget		
try		
start		
allow		

With Change in Meaning

Some verbs can take either a gerund or an infinitive but the meanings of the sentences differ. Consider the following two sentences:

I stopped to eat. —> I stopped doing something in order to eat.
I stopped eating. —> I was eating, and then I stopped.

Other verbs that can use either a gerund or an infinitive with a change in meaning are the following:

remember, regret, forget, try

What's the difference in meaning?

If you remember to call me, I will take you out to dinner.
(Call me in the future, and I'll take you to dinner.)

If you remember calling me, I will take you out to dinner.
(You called me before. Do you remember? If you remember having done so, I'll take you to dinner!)

You should remember to call your friend. (later)
I don't remember calling my friend. (in the past)

I regret to say it, but you are too nice. (Regret comes before the comment/
    expressing my feeling about you - now)

I regret saying that you are too nice.
(Regret comes after the comment/I made the comment in the past.
But now I regret saying it.)

I regret to inform you that we cannot bring you on board. (I'm sorry I have to say this now)
I regret informing you about the result. (I'm sorry about telling you the results
                                        - in the past)

Don't forget to mail the letter.
(You should mail the letter later)

I'll never forget mailing a letter to the president.
(The mailing has already been done.)

Here is a list of verbs for which you can use both the gerund and the infinitive, but with a possible change in meaning.

Verb	Gerund sentence	Infinitive sentence
forget		
go on		
mean		
regret		
remember		
stop		
try		
like		
afraid		
need		
used to		

Prepositional Phrases followed by Gerunds

Prepositional Phrase	Make sentences
get through to	
in addition to	
apologize (to someone) for	
be committed to	
dream of	
forgive (someone) for	
instead of	
look forward to	
prevent (someone) from	
stop (someone) from	
take advantage of	
thank (someone) for	
be tired of	
be accustomed to	
be afraid of	
tired of	

Prepositional Phrase	Make sentences
blame (someone) for	
be capable of	
complain about	
be excited about	
be guilty of	
be interested in	
be opposed to	
be scared of	
succeed in	
be terrified of	
think of	
admit to	
disagree with	
aim at	
disapprove of	
replete with	

STEP 24

Subject-Verb Agreement

Subject-verb agrement is one of the most common errors learners of English make, along with the use of wrong tenses. Let's consider a simple example.

The cat is *sleeping on the couch.*
The cats are *sleeping on the couch.*

The general rule is that if the subject is singular the verb should be singular, and if the subject is plural, the verb should be plural.

What about the following?

    The police is/are keeping my neighborhood safe.
        Correct: The police are keeping my neighborhood safe.

    Every Tom, Dick, and Harry need/needs to be careful about overeating.
    Correct: Every Tom, Dick, and Harry needs to be careful about overeating.

    Every is followed by a singular noun (every country, every station, every night).
    For every and each, use singular verb.

    Each tree and flower is/are labeled.
        Which is correct?

    The pictures on that wall is/are amazing.
        Which is correct?

What about the following?

One hundred dollars is/are a lot of money.
> Correct: One hundred dollars is a lot of money.

Why? The reason is that in some cases, such as time and money, the amount involved is considered as a whole, as one.

Subject-Verb Agreement

1) The people who made this artwork *is/are* military veterans.

2) The amount of water they put into the containers *is/are* staggering.

3) Bananas, pineapples, and mangoes *is/are* healthy for you.

4) Why *does/do* James and Akemi always finish each other's sentences?

5) Each of the students *has/have* to bring a notebook to school.

6) Some of the fruit in the large cup *is/are* yellow.

7) Some of the fruits in the bucket *is/are* ripe.

8) A lot of the equipment on the site *is/are* rusty.

9) Some of the clothing in the shop *is/are* tattered.

10) Some of the movie *is/are* exciting.

11) One of my professors *is/are* on the second floor.

12) Part of the money *is/are* in the bank.

13) A number of people *is/are* talking about having a party.

14) The number of people coming to the party *is/are* large.

14) None of the furniture *was/were* made in Japan.

15) None of the stories *is/are* true.

16) The United States *is/are* not the largest country in the world.

17) The news coming out of the Middle East *is/are* encouraging.

18) 10,000 kilometers *is/are* as far as the spacecraft can go.

19) The Chinese *drinks/drink* a lot of tea.

20) Ten hours *is/are* more than enough sleep.

21) Three times three *is/are* nine.

22) Mumps *is/are* a terrible disease.

23) The United Nations *has/have* a university in Tokyo.

23) A red bird and a yellow bird *is/are* sitting on the tree branch.

24) A red and yellow bird *is/are* sitting on the tree branch.

25) A professor and an author *is/are* having dinner at the Ritz-Carlton.

26) A professor and author *is/are* having dinner at the Ritz-Carlton.

STEP 25

Idiomatic Expressions - #1

(Note that some expressions have both a literal and metaphorical meaning.)

1.

Idiom	turn up the heat
Meaning	
Sample sentence/ My sentence	

2.

Idiom	wild goose chase
Meaning	
Sample sentence/ My sentence	

3.

Idiom	muddy the waters
Meaning	
Sample sentence/ My sentence	

4.

Idiom	a witch hunt
Meaning	
Sample sentence/ My sentence	

5.

Idiom	a balancing act
Meaning	
Sample sentence/ My sentence	

6.

Idiom	get carried away
Meaning	
Sample sentence/ My sentence	

7.

Idiom	a race to the bottom
Meaning	
Sample sentence/ My sentence	

8.

Idiom	weigh in
Meaning	
Sample sentence/ My sentence	

9.

Idiom	a ton of money
Meaning	
Sample sentence/ My sentence	

10.

Idiom	hollow out
Meaning	
Sample sentence/ My sentence	

11.

Idiom	one's own worst enemy
Meaning	
Sample sentence/ My sentence	

12.

Idiom	red line
Meaning	
Sample sentence/ My sentence	

13.

Idiom	meltdown
Meaning	
Sample sentence/ My sentence	

14.

Idiom	have somebody's blood on your hands
Meaning	
Sample sentence/ My sentence	

15.

Idiom	go with one's gut
Meaning	
Sample sentence/ My sentence	

16.

Idiom	stop the bleeding
Meaning	
Sample sentence/ My sentence	

17.

Idiom	silver lining
Meaning	
Sample sentence/ My sentence	

18.

Idiom	take the high road
Meaning	
Sample sentence/ My sentence	

19.

Idiom	trip over oneself
Meaning	
Sample sentence/ My sentence	

20.

Idiom	run someone/something to ground
Meaning	
Sample sentence/ My sentence	

21.

Idiom	Debbie Downer
Meaning	
Sample sentence/ My sentence	

22.

Idiom	all over the map
Meaning	
Sample sentence/ My sentence	

23.

Idiom	go on the offensive
Meaning	
Sample sentence/ My sentence	

24.

Idiom	in great spirits
Meaning	
Sample sentence/ My sentence	

STEP 26
Word Forms - #5: Nouns, Verbs & Adjectives

1.

		Make sentences to demonstrate your understanding of the differences in usage
Noun	avoidance	
Verb	avoid	
Adjective	avoidable	

2.

		Make sentences to demonstrate your understanding of the differences in usage
Noun	belief	
Verb	believe	
Adjective	believable	

3.

		Make sentences to demonstrate your understanding of the differences in usage
Noun	blackness	
Verb	blacken	
Adjective	black	

4.

		Make sentences to demonstrate your understanding of the differences in usage
Noun	blood	
Verb	bleed	
Adjective	bloody	

5.

		Make sentences to demonstrate your understanding of the differences in usage
Noun	boredom	
Verb	bore	
Adjective	boring	

6.

		Make sentences to demonstrate your understanding of the differences in usage
Noun	bother	
Verb	bother	
Adjective	bothersome	

7.

		Make sentences to demonstrate your understanding of the differences in usage
Noun	nullification	
Verb	nullify	
Adjective	nullified	

8.

		Make sentences to demonstrate your understanding of the differences in usage
Noun	burial	
Verb	bury	
Adjective	buried	

9.

		Make sentences to demonstrate your understanding of the differences in usage
Noun	care	
Verb	care	
Adjective	careful	

10.

		Make sentences to demonstrate your understanding of the differences in usage
Noun	challenge	
Verb	challenge	
Adjective	challenging	

11.

		Make sentences to demonstrate your understanding of the differences in usage
Noun	chase	
Verb	chase	
Adjective	chasing	

12.

		Make sentences to demonstrate your understanding of the differences in usage
Noun	choice	
Verb	choose	
Adjective	chosen	

13.

		Make sentences to demonstrate your understanding of the differences in usage
Noun	clarity	
Verb	clear	
Adjective	clear	

14.

		Make sentences to demonstrate your understanding of the differences in usage
Noun	collection	
Verb	collect	
Adjective	collective	

15.

		Make sentences to demonstrate your understanding of the differences in usage
Noun	repudiation	
Verb	repudiate	
Adjective	repudiated	

STEP 27
Transitive and Intransitive Verbs

Imagine watching television when someone comes on the screen and says, "The hunter killed!" What question would you ask yourself?

The hunter killed **what**?

In this case, the verb "kill" is in transit; it has not arrived at its destination. The speaker has to complete the "journey" of the sentence by mentioning the object that was killed. We can ask the question, "What?" or "Who?" to help us get the answer to the object.

And the reply might be, "The hunter killed a lion."

"Kill" in this case is a transitive verb and the sentence comes in the form,

subject	+	**verb**	+	**object**
The hunter		killed		a lion

What about the following?

The student **raised**. You will ask, "The student raised **what**?" And the answer might be, "The student raised **her hand**." "Raise," therefore, is a transitive verb.

Intransitive Verbs (subject + verb)

Intransitive verbs usually involve one subject, that is, one person or thing taking action. This is not action taken against something else or someone else.

For example,

>I sat (in the chair) (for an hour.)
>Subject (I) + verb (sat)
>
>The train departed.
>The shop opened.
>The people came.
>His arm weakened.
>The bus arrived.

All of these can be expanded by adding some more information but they do not answer the question "What?" or "Who?".

>The train departed on time.
>The shop opened again.
>The people came with their instruments.
>His arm weakened considerably.
>The bus arrived late.

Keep in mind that some verbs can be used both transitively and intransitively. So, when you check for the meaning of a word in a dictionary, check to see if it has the label transitive (tr.) or intransitive (int.). Some dictionaries will give you separate definitions, along with examples of how you can use the word either transitively or intransitively. It's important to be aware of the different ways in which words behave.

a) I write in my diary every day. (I write what? It does not say - intransitive)
b) I write essays every day. (I write what? Essays - transitive)

Common Transitive Verbs: Make sentences

1. write

2. sell

3. see

4. forget

5. find

6. get

7. drink

8. help

9. stop

10. meet

11. pay

12. sing

13. bring

14. sell

15. eat

16. break

17. like

18. answer

19. buy

20. carry

21. take

22. give

23. understand

24. clean

Common Intransitive Verbs: Make Sentences

1. weep

2. sleep

3. stand

4. lie

5. remain

6. jump

7. cough

8. fall

9. flow

10. kneel

11. travel

12. die

13. fly

14. walk

15. dance

16. wait

17. belong

18. come

19. go

20. sit

21. cry

22. laugh

23. talk

STEP 28
Verbs - #3

Make a sentence with each of the following verbs:

1. mend

2. pack

3. expose

4. catch

5. topple

6. crash

7. deliver

8. seize

9. tumble

10. pull

11. swing

12. unfurl

13. push

14. release

15. pierce

16. deliver

17. push

18. rush

19. dash

20. expand

21. peel

22. slide

23. display

24. build

25. attend

26. leap

27. skip

28. splice

29. toss

30. swing

STEP 29
Participial Adjectives - #1: Are You Boring or Just Bored?

You've probably heard someone saying, "I am boring." Even though you might have agreed with the person, you probably sensed that what the person really wanted to say was that she was bored.

Something is boring. So, I am bored.
Something is exciting. So, I am excited.
Something is surprising. So, I am excited.
Something is fascinating. So, I am fascinated.
Something is interesting. So, I am interested.
Something is shocking. So, I am shocked.
Something is tiring. So, I am tired.

From Verbs to Adjectives

You notice that all the above words used to describe how you felt are verbs (bore, excite, surprise, fascinate, interest, shock, tire).

The present participle form (...ing) describes what produced the feeling and the past participle form (...ed) describes how you or your friends or someone felt.

If a person is the source of the feeling, then it is correct to use the ...ing form to describe the person. For example, "My teacher is so boring on Monday mornings, but very exciting on Friday evenings."

Participial Adjectives

Make one sentence for each pair of words, showing the event or person/people that produced the feeling and who experienced the feeling.

Participial Adjectives	Make sentences
alarming, alarmed	
aggravating, aggravated	
amazing, amazed	
amusing, amused	
astonishing, astonished	
bewildering, bewildered	
captivating, captivated	

Participial Adjectives	Make sentences
astonishing, astonished	
comforting, comforted	
concerning, concerned	
confusing, confused	
convincing, convinced	
depressing, depressed	
devastating, devastated	

Participial Adjectives	Make sentences
disappointing, disappointed	
discouraging, discouraged	
distressing, distressed	
encouraging, encouraged	
energizing, energized	
disturbing, distressed	
enraging, enraged	
embarrassing, embarrassed	

STEP 30
Word Forms - #6: Nouns, Verbs, & Adjectives

1.

		Make sentences to demonstrate your understanding of the differences in usage
Noun	comfort	
Verb	comfort	
Adjective	comfortable	

2.

		Make sentences to demonstrate your understanding of the differences in usage
Noun	laceration	
Verb	lacerate	
Adjective	lacerated	

3.

		Make sentences to demonstrate your understanding of the differences in usage
Noun	confusion	
Verb	confuse	
Adjective	confused	

4.

		Make sentences to demonstrate your understanding of the differences in usage
Noun	consideration	
Verb	consider	
Adjective	considerable/ considerate	

5.

		Make sentences to demonstrate your understanding of the differences in usage
Noun	consolation	
Verb	console	
Adjective	consoled	

6.

		Make sentences to demonstrate your understanding of the differences in usage
Noun	continuity/ continuation	
Verb	continue	
Adjective	continuous/ continual	

7.

		Make sentences to demonstrate your understanding of the differences in usage
Noun	craze	
Verb	craze	
Adjective	crazy	

8.

	Make sentences to demonstrate your understanding of the differences in usage
Noun	creation	
Verb	create	
Adjective	creative	

9.

	Make sentences to demonstrate your understanding of the differences in usage
Noun	dedication	
Verb	dedicate	
Adjective	dedicated	

10.

	Make sentences to demonstrate your understanding of the differences in usage
Noun	cure	
Verb	cure	
Adjective	curable	

11.

	Make sentences to demonstrate your understanding of the differences in usage
Noun	curse	
Verb	curse	
Adjective	cursed	

12.

		Make sentences to demonstrate your understanding of the differences in usage
Noun	damage	
Verb	damage	
Adjective	damaged/ damaging	

13.

		Make sentences to demonstrate your understanding of the differences in usage
Noun	deafness	
Verb	deafen	
Adjective	deafening/ deaf	

14.

		Make sentences to demonstrate your understanding of the differences in usage
Noun	decision	
Verb	decide	
Adjective	decisive	

15.

		Make sentences to demonstrate your understanding of the differences in usage
Noun	abstention	
Verb	abstain	
Adjective	abstemious	

16.

		Make sentences to demonstrate your understanding of the differences in usage
Noun	enunciation	
Verb	enunciate	
Adjective	enunciatory/ enunciated	

17.

		Make sentences to demonstrate your understanding of the differences in usage
Noun	rescindment	
Verb	rescind	
Adjective	rescindable	

18.

		Make sentences to demonstrate your understanding of the differences in usage
Noun	lamentation	
Verb	lament	
Adjective	lamentable	

19.

		Make sentences to demonstrate your understanding of the differences in usage
Noun	resonance	
Verb	resonate	
Adjective	resonant	

20.

		Make sentences to demonstrate your understanding of the differences in usage
Noun	acceleration	
Verb	accelerate	
Adjective	accelerant	

21.

		Make sentences to demonstrate your understanding of the differences in usage
Noun	arrogation	
Verb	arrogate	
Adjective	arrogant	

22.

		Make sentences to demonstrate your understanding of the differences in usage
Noun	endowment	
Verb	endow	
Adjective	endowed	

23.

		Make sentences to demonstrate your understanding of the differences in usage
Noun	intensification	
Verb	intensify	
Adjective	intensified	

STEP 31
Verb Tenses - #2

Complete the following table. Check the meanings of words you do not know.

Verb Tenses			
No.	Verb	Past tense	Past Participle
1	Kneel		
2	Know		
3	Lay		
4	Lead		
5	Lean		
6	Leap		
7	Learn		
8	Leave		
9	Lend		
10	Let		
11	Lie (down)		

Verb Tenses

No.	Verb	Past tense	Past Participle
12	Lip-read		
13	Lose		
14	Make		
15	Mean		
16	Meet		
17	Melt		
18	Misgive		
19	Mislay		
20	Misread		
21	Misspeak		
22	Misspend		
23	Mistake		
24	Misunderstand		
25	Miswrite		
26	Mow		

Verb Tenses

No.	Verb	Past tense	Past Participle
27	Nose-dive		
28	Offset		
29	Oppose		
30	Outbid		
31	Outdo		
32	Outdraw		
33	Outdrink		
34	Outgrow		
35	Output		
36	Outrun		
37	Outsell		
38	Outshine		
39	Overbid		
40	Overblow		
41	Overbuild		

Verb Tenses

No.	Verb	Past tense	Past Participle
42	Overbuy		
43	Overcome		
44	Overdo		
45	Overdraw		
46	Overdrink		
47	Overeat		
48	Overfeed		
49	Overfly		
50	Overhear		
51	Overwrite		
52	Overleap		
53	Overlearn		
54	Overpay		
55	Override		
56	Overrun		

Verb Tenses			
No.	Verb	Past tense	Past Participle
57	Oversee		
58	Oversell		
59	Overset		
60	Overshoot		
61	Oversleep		
62	Overspend		
63	Overtake		
64	Overthink		
65	Partake		
66	Pay		
67	Pen		
68	Pinch-hit		
69	Plead		
70	Prebuild		
71	Precut		

Verb Tenses

No.	Verb	Past tense	Past Participle
71	Prepay		
72	Presell		
73	Preset		
74	Preshrink		
75	Proofread		
76	Prove		
77	Put		
78	Quick-freeze		
79	Quit		
80	Reprove		
81	Read		
82	Reawake		
83	Rebind		
84	Rebuild		
85	Revoke		

STEP 32

Idiomatic Expressions - #2

1.

Idiom	giant killer
Meaning	
Sample sentence/ My sentence	

2.

Idiom	flesh (something) out
Meaning	
Sample sentence/ My sentence	

3.

Idiom	skunk at the garden party
Meaning	
Sample sentence/ My sentence	

4.

Idiom	gain steam
Meaning	
Sample sentence/ My sentence	

5.

Idiom	go off the rails
Meaning	
Sample sentence/ My sentence	

6.

Idiom	hit rock bottom
Meaning	
Sample sentence/ My sentence	

7.

Idiom	cut ties with (someone)
Meaning	
Sample sentence/ My sentence	

8.

Idiom	send a message
Meaning	
Sample sentence/ My sentence	

9.

Idiom	throw (one's) hat into the ring
Meaning	
Sample sentence/ My sentence	

10.

Idiom	a runaway train
Meaning	
Sample sentence/ My sentence	

11.

Idiom	know where all the bodies are buried
Meaning	
Sample sentence/ My sentence	

12.

Idiom	squeaky clean
Meaning	
Sample sentence/ My sentence	

13.

Idiom	tip of the iceberg
Meaning	
Sample sentence/ My sentence	

14.

Idiom	in deep water
Meaning	
Sample sentence/ My sentence	

15.

Idiom	throw stones
Meaning	
Sample sentence/ My sentence	

16.

Idiom	rub (someone) the wrong way
Meaning	
Sample sentence/ My sentence	

17.

Idiom	take it on the chin
Meaning	
Sample sentence/ My sentence	

18.

Idiom	backlash
Meaning	
Sample sentence/ My sentence	

19.

Idiom	blow (one's) mind
Meaning	
Sample sentence/ My sentence	

20.

Idiom	pour cold water on (something)
Meaning	
Sample sentence/ My sentence	

21.

Idiom	word of the mouth
Meaning	
Sample sentence/ My sentence	

22.

Idiom	reinvent (oneself)
Meaning	
Sample sentence/ My sentence	

23.

Idiom	fan the flames
Meaning	
Sample sentence/ My sentence	

24.

Idiom	sucker for someone or something
Meaning	
Sample sentence/ My sentence	

24.

Idiom	bring home the bacon
Meaning	
Sample sentence/ My sentence	

24.

Idiom	a hot potato
Meaning	
Sample sentence/ My sentence	

24.

Idiom	miss the boat
Meaning	
Sample sentence/ My sentence	

24.

Idiom	slip of the tongue
Meaning	
Sample sentence/ My sentence	

24.

Idiom	tongue in cheek
Meaning	
Sample sentence/ My sentence	

STEP 33
Prepositional Phrases

It is useful to learn about prepositions and how they combine with verbs, nouns, and adjectives to create standard phrases that appear again and again in the language. Often, when you know the correct combination of words, it is easy to eliminate answers that are the wrong combination. Whereas, when you do not know what is right, it is easy to multiply your confusion when you see combinations that sound good but may not be right.

Make sentences with the following phrases. If you do not know the meaning, please do some research.

Phrase	My sentence
decrease in	
be worried about	
be absent from	
be pleased with	
vote for	
be accustomed to	
be used to	
distinguish from	
be jealous of	
be disappointed in	

Phrase	My sentence
victims of	
be acquainted with	
be tired of	
be addicted to	
be upset with	
be afraid of	
think of	
agree with	
thank for	
be angry with	
be terrified of	
become numb to	
talk about	
apply to	
talk of	
be terrified by	
be angry at	
be tired from	

STEP 34
Word Forms - #7: Nouns, Verbs, & Adjectives

1.

		Make sentences to demonstrate your understanding of the differences in usage
Noun	decoration	
Verb	decorate	
Adjective	decorative	

2.

		Make sentences to demonstrate your understanding of the differences in usage
Noun	demand	
Verb	demand	
Adjective	demanding	

3.

		Make sentences to demonstrate your understanding of the differences in usage
Noun	derivation	
Verb	derive	
Adjective	derivative	

4.

		Make sentences to demonstrate your understanding of the differences in usage
Noun	deservedness	
Verb	deserve	
Adjective	deserving	

5.

		Make sentences to demonstrate your understanding of the differences in usage
Noun	destruction	
Verb	destroy	
Adjective	destructive	

6.

		Make sentences to demonstrate your understanding of the differences in usage
Noun	development	
Verb	develop	
Adjective	developing/ developed	

7.

		Make sentences to demonstrate your understanding of the differences in usage
Noun	death	
Verb	die	
Adjective	dead	

8.

		Make sentences to demonstrate your understanding of the differences in usage
Noun	difference	
Verb	differ	
Adjective	different	

9.

		Make sentences to demonstrate your understanding of the differences in usage
Noun	disturbance	
Verb	disturb	
Adjective	disturbing/ disturbed	

10.

		Make sentences to demonstrate your understanding of the differences in usage
Noun	dust	
Verb	dust	
Adjective	dusty	

11.

		Make sentences to demonstrate your understanding of the differences in usage
Noun	education	
Verb	educate	
Adjective	educative/ educable	

12.

		Make sentences to demonstrate your understanding of the differences in usage
Noun	embarrassment	
Verb	embarrass	
Adjective	embarrassing	

13.

		Make sentences to demonstrate your understanding of the differences in usage
Noun	emptiness	
Verb	empty	
Adjective	empty	

14.

		Make sentences to demonstrate your understanding of the differences in usage
Noun	circle	
Verb	encircle	
Adjective	circular	

15.

		Make sentences to demonstrate your understanding of the differences in usage
Noun	maximum	
Verb	maximize	
Adjective	maximum/ maximal	

16.

		Make sentences to demonstrate your understanding of the differences in usage
Noun	cooperation	
Verb	cooperate	
Adjective	cooperative	

17.

		Make sentences to demonstrate your understanding of the differences in usage
Noun	concurrence	
Verb	concur	
Adjective	concurrent	

18.

		Make sentences to demonstrate your understanding of the differences in usage
Noun	documentation	
Verb	document	
Adjective	documented	

19.

		Make sentences to demonstrate your understanding of the differences in usage
Noun	preference	
Verb	prefer	
Adjective	preferred	

20.

		Make sentences to demonstrate your understanding of the differences in usage
Noun	production	
Verb	produce	
Adjective	productive	

21.

		Make sentences to demonstrate your understanding of the differences in usage
Noun	justification	
Verb	justify	
Adjective	justified	

22.

		Make sentences to demonstrate your understanding of the differences in usage
Noun	distraction	
Verb	distract	
Adjective	distracting	

23.

		Make sentences to demonstrate your understanding of the differences in usage
Noun	benefit/ beneficiary	
Verb	benefit	
Adjective	beneficial	

24.

		Make sentences to demonstrate your understanding of the differences in usage
Noun	cultivation	
Verb	cultivate	
Adjective	cultivated	

25.

		Make sentences to demonstrate your understanding of the differences in usage
Noun	remnant	
Verb	remain	
Adjective	remnant/ remaining	

26.

		Make sentences to demonstrate your understanding of the differences in usage
Noun	modification	
Verb	modify	
Adjective	modified/ modifying	

27.

		Make sentences to demonstrate your understanding of the differences in usage
Noun	identification	
Verb	identify	
Adjective	identifying/ identified	

28.

		Make sentences to demonstrate your understanding of the differences in usage
Noun	denigration	
Verb	denigrate	
Adjective	denigratory/ denigrative	

29.

		Make sentences to demonstrate your understanding of the differences in usage
Noun	correction	
Verb	correct	
Adjective	correct/ corrective	

30.

		Make sentences to demonstrate your understanding of the differences in usage
Noun	threat	
Verb	threaten	
Adjective	threatening	

31.

		Make sentences to demonstrate your understanding of the differences in usage
Noun	refutation	
Verb	refute	
Adjective	refutable	

32.

		Make sentences to demonstrate your understanding of the differences in usage
Noun	conclusion	
Verb	conclude	
Adjective	conclusive	

33.

		Make sentences to demonstrate your understanding of the differences in usage
Noun	corrosion	
Verb	corrode	
Adjective	corrosive	

34.

		Make sentences to demonstrate your understanding of the differences in usage
Noun	analysis	
Verb	analyze	
Adjective	analyzable/ analyzed	

35.

		Make sentences to demonstrate your understanding of the differences in usage
Noun	addition	
Verb	add	
Adjective	added	

STEP 35

Participial Adjectives - #2

As you did before, make a sentence for each pair of words in which you show what event or person caused the feeling and who experienced the feeling.

Participial Adjectives	Make sentences
entertaining, entertained	
exasperating, exasperated	
exhausting, exhausted	
flattering, flattered	
compelling, compelled	

Participial Adjectives	Make sentences
frustrating, frustrated	
fulfilling, fulfilled	
gratifying, gratified	
humiliating, humiliated	
inspiring, inspired	
insulting, insulted	
intriguing, intrigued	

Participial Adjectives	Make sentences
mystifying, mystified	
moving, moved	
overwhelming, overwhelmed	
perplexing, perplexed	
perturbing, perturbed	
pleasing, pleased	
puzzling, puzzled	

Participial Adjectives	Make sentences
frightening, frightened	
relaxing, relaxed	
satisfying, satisfied	
sickening, sickened	
soothing, soothed	
tempting, tempted	
terrifying, terrified	

Participial Adjectives	Make sentences
threatening, threatened	
thrilling, thrilled	
touching, touched	
unnerving, unnerved	
troubling, troubled	
unsettling, unsettled	
upsetting, upset	

STEP 36

House & Home

House and Home items frequently feature in the listening section of the TOEIC. Of course, such words can also appear in the reading section. When that happens you do not want the test to be the first time you encounter a word. Being familiar with a word and being able to use it correctly puts you in a better position to both recognize it and to figure out if it is the answer you need to choose or one that you should reject.

Use the following household words and items in sentences of your own to demonstrate your understanding of their meanings.

1. shelf

2. curtain

3. vase

4. carpet

5. fireplace

6. window shade

7. cushion

8. window

9. piano keys

10. candle

11. plant

12. awnings

13. wall

14. mantel

15. lintel

16. chair

17. floor

18. ceiling

19. roof

20. piano bench

21. sports equipment

22. electronics

23. appliances

24. entryway

25. attic

26. dining room

27. laundry room

28. exercise equipment

29. children's toys

30. bicycles

31. high chair

32. necklace

33. earrings

34. gaming system

35. computer accessories

36. musical instruments

37. figurines

38. antiques

39. clothing

40. power tools

41. lawn mower

42. refrigerator

43. dishwasher

44. sump pump

45. rug

46. furniture

47. closet

48. sewing machine

49. dresser

50. chest

51. lamp

52. blinds

53. cabinet

54. linen

55. stove

56. silverware

57. ironing board

58. glassware

59. portable dishwasher

60. organ

61. mirror

STEP 37

Verb Tenses - #3

Complete the following table. Check the meanings of words you do not know.

Verb Tenses			
No.	Verb	Past tense	Past Participle
1	Spill		
2	Spin		
3	Spit		
4	Split		
5	Spoil		
6	Spoon-feed		
7	Spread		
8	Spring		
9	Stand		
10	Stave		
11	Steal		

Verb Tenses			
No.	Verb	Past tense	Past Participle
12	Stick		
13	Sting		
14	Stink		
15	Strew		
16	Stride		
17	Strike		
18	String		
19	Strip		
20	Strive		
21	Sublet		
22	Sunburn		
23	Swear		
24	Sweat		
25	Sweep		
26	Swell		

Verb Tenses			
No.	Verb	Past tense	Past Participle
27	Swim		
28	Swing		
29	Take		
30	Teach		
31	Team-teach		
32	Tear		
33	Telecast		
34	Tell		
35	Test-drive		
36	Test-fly		
37	Think		
38	Throw		
39	Thrust		
40	Tread		
41	Troubleshoot		

Verb Tenses			
No.	Verb	Past tense	Past Participle
42	Typecast		
43	Typeset		
44	Typewrite		
45	Unbend		
46	Unbind		
47	Unclothe		
48	Underbid		
49	Underbuy		
50	Undercut		
51	Underdo		
52	Underfeed		
53	Undergird		
54	Undergo		
55	Underlay		
56	Underlie		

STEP 38
Word Forms - #8: Nouns, Verbs, & Adjectives

1.

		Make sentences to demonstrate your understanding of the differences in usage
Noun	encouragement	
Verb	encourage	
Adjective	encouraging	

2.

		Make sentences to demonstrate your understanding of the differences in usage
Noun	danger	
Verb	endanger	
Adjective	dangerous	

3.

		Make sentences to demonstrate your understanding of the differences in usage
Noun	enthusiasm	
Verb	enthuse	
Adjective	enthusiastic	

4.

		Make sentences to demonstrate your understanding of the differences in usage
Noun	number	
Verb	enumerate	
Adjective	numerable/ numerous	

5.

		Make sentences to demonstrate your understanding of the differences in usage
Noun	envy	
Verb	envy	
Adjective	envious	

6.

		Make sentences to demonstrate your understanding of the differences in usage
Noun	evaporation	
Verb	evaporate	
Adjective	evaporating/ evaporated	

7.

		Make sentences to demonstrate your understanding of the differences in usage
Noun	expectation	
Verb	expect	
Adjective	expected/ expecting	

8.

		Make sentences to demonstrate your understanding of the differences in usage
Noun	explanation	
Verb	explain	
Adjective	explainable	

9.

		Make sentences to demonstrate your understanding of the differences in usage
Noun	exploration	
Verb	explore	
Adjective	explorable	

10.

		Make sentences to demonstrate your understanding of the differences in usage
Noun	food	
Verb	feed	
Adjective	food	

11.

		Make sentences to demonstrate your understanding of the differences in usage
Noun	firmness	
Verb	firm	
Adjective	firm	

12.

		Make sentences to demonstrate your understanding of the differences in usage
Noun	fascination	
Verb	fascinate	
Adjective	fascinating/ fascinated	

13.

		Make sentences to demonstrate your understanding of the differences in usage
Noun	flight	
Verb	fly	
Adjective	flying	

14.

		Make sentences to demonstrate your understanding of the differences in usage
Noun	harm	
Verb	harm	
Adjective	harmful	

15.

		Make sentences to demonstrate your understanding of the differences in usage
Noun	detection	
Verb	detect	
Adjective	detected/ detective	

16.

		Make sentences to demonstrate your understanding of the differences in usage
Noun	conversion	
Verb	convert	
Adjective	converted	

17.

		Make sentences to demonstrate your understanding of the differences in usage
Noun	condensation	
Verb	condense	
Adjective	condensed	

18.

		Make sentences to demonstrate your understanding of the differences in usage
Noun	departure	
Verb	depart	
Adjective	departed/ departing	

19.

		Make sentences to demonstrate your understanding of the differences in usage
Noun	complication	
Verb	complicate	
Adjective	complicated	

20.

		Make sentences to demonstrate your understanding of the differences in usage
Noun	connection	
Verb	connect	
Adjective	connective/ connected	

21.

		Make sentences to demonstrate your understanding of the differences in usage
Noun	change	
Verb	change	
Adjective	changeable/ changed	

22.

		Make sentences to demonstrate your understanding of the differences in usage
Noun	requirement	
Verb	require	
Adjective	required	

23.

		Make sentences to demonstrate your understanding of the differences in usage
Noun	evolution	
Verb	evolve	
Adjective	evolving	

24.

		Make sentences to demonstrate your understanding of the differences in usage
Noun	revolution revolt	
Verb	revolt	
Adjective	revolutionary / revolting	

25.

		Make sentences to demonstrate your understanding of the differences in usage
Noun	infuriation	
Verb	infuriate	
Adjective	infuriating/ infuriated	

26.

		Make sentences to demonstrate your understanding of the differences in usage
Noun	eviction	
Verb	evict	
Adjective	evicted	

27.

		Make sentences to demonstrate your understanding of the differences in usage
Noun	exclusion	
Verb	exclude	
Adjective	exclusive	

28.

		Make sentences to demonstrate your understanding of the differences in usage
Noun	exculpation	
Verb	exculpate	
Adjective	exculpatory	

29.

		Make sentences to demonstrate your understanding of the differences in usage
Noun	preclusion	
Verb	preclude	
Adjective	preclusive	

30.

		Make sentences to demonstrate your understanding of the differences in usage
Noun	probe	
Verb	probe	
Adjective	probing	

31.

		Make sentences to demonstrate your understanding of the differences in usage
Noun	frustration	
Verb	frustrate	
Adjective	frustrated	

STEP 39

More Prepositional Phrases

Demonstrate your understanding of the following phrases by forming sentences with each of them.

Phrase	My sentence
consist of	
participate in	
be content with	
decide on	
be convinced of	
be proud of	
be coordinated with	
count on	
count upon	
be disappointed with	
be protected from	
be patient with	

Phrase	My sentence
prohibit from	
be covered with	
be crowded with	
prevent from	
decide upon	
be dedicated to	
be prepared for	
depend on	
pray for	
be devoted to	
be polite to	
be disappointed in	
be pleased with	
depend upon	
be discriminated against	
introduce to	
be divorced from	

Phrase	My sentence
be interested in	
insist on	
be done with	
keep from	
be known for	
be located in	
look forward to	
be made from	
object to	
be married to	
be made of	
be disappointed with	
connected to	
rescue from	
be aware of	
be blessed with	
compare with	

Phrase	My sentence
be remembered for	
be bored by	
be qualified for	
rely on	
blame for	
be bored with	
rely upon	
care for	
provide with	
recover from	
be concerned about	
complain of	
be composed of	
entitled to	
commensurate with	
suited to	
lead to	

STEP 40
Prefixes - #1

The more words you know, the easier it is for you to understand what you hear or read. So, making an effort to expand your vocabulary on a daily basis is important. One way to accelerate this process is to learn about prefixes and suffixes. In this unit, we will focus on prefixes, and in later units, on suffixes.

In simple terms, from the table below, the stem is the main part of a word. The prefix is a particle that you attach in front of the stem, while the suffix is a particle that you attach to the back.

Prefix	Stem	Suffix
un-	reliable	-ly
un-	intention	-al

If you know the meanings of these prefixes and suffixes, you can considerably expand your vocabulary. On the other hand, if you do not have a good understanding of these prefixes and suffixes, you place yourself at a great disadvantage as far as your understanding of English is concerned.

Prefixes

Prefix / Meaning	Example words	Find the Meanings
a-, ab-, abs- away from, away, off, departing from, differing from	absent	
	abscond	
	abseiling	
	abnormal	
	abnegate	

Prefix / Meaning	Example words	Find the meanings
ad-, a-, ac-, af-, ag-, an-, ar-, at-, as- to, toward	adapt	
	adhere	
	annex	
	attract	
	acknowledge	

Prefix / Meaning	Example words	Find the Meanings
anti-, ant-, against, opposite in kind, position, or action, contrary,	antisocial	
	antifreeze	
	antagonist	
	antiseptic	
	antipathy	

Prefix / Meaning	Example words	Find the Meanings
bi-, bis- two	biped	
	bicycle	
	binomial	
	biennial	
	bipartisan	

Use each of the following words to form a sentence.

1. abandon

2. abase

3. abate

4. abbreviate

5. abdicate

6. adopt

7. addict

8. adept

9. adhere

10. antiaging

11. antibacterial

12. antibiotic

13. anticipate

14. anticlotting

15. antidote

16. antismoking

17. binoculars

18. bisect

19. antedate

20. antecedent

21. audiotape

22. audiovisual

23. auditorium

24. audience

25. autopilot

26. automatic

27. autobiography

28. disagree

29. midweek

30. distrust

31. misplace

32. misbehave

STEP 41

Verb Tenses - #4

Complete the Following Table.

Check the meanings of words you do not know.

Verb Tenses			
No.	Verb	Past tense	Past Participle
1	Wake		
2	Waylay		
3	Wear		
4	Weave		
5	Wed		
6	Weep		
7	Wend		
8	Underpay		
9	Underrun		
10	Undersell		
11	Undershoot		

Verb Tenses			
No.	Verb	Past tense	Past Participle
12	Underspend		
13	Understand		
14	Undertake		
15	Underwrite		
16	Undo		
17	Unlearn		
18	Unmake		
19	Unstick		
20	Unweave		
21	Unwind		
22	Upbuild		
23	Uphold		
24	Upset		
25	Vex		
26	Wet		

Verb Tenses			
No.	Verb	Past tense	Past Participle
27	Win		
28	Wind		
29	Withdraw		
30	Withhold		
31	Withstand		
32	Work		
33	Wrap		
34	Wreak		
35	Wring		
36	Write		
37	Weave		
38	Lasso		
39	Debut		
40	Bow		
41	Unveil		

STEP 42
Word Forms - #9: Nouns, Verbs, & Adjectives

1.

		Make sentences to demonstrate your understanding of the differences in usage
Noun	force	
Verb	force	
Adjective	forceful	

2.

		Make sentences to demonstrate your understanding of the differences in usage
Noun	glory	
Verb	glorify	
Adjective	glorious	

3.

		Make sentences to demonstrate your understanding of the differences in usage
Noun	health	
Verb	heal	
Adjective	healthy	

4.

		Make sentences to demonstrate your understanding of the differences in usage
Noun	hope	
Verb	hope	
Adjective	hopeful	

5.

		Make sentences to demonstrate your understanding of the differences in usage
Noun	identification	
Verb	identify	
Adjective	identifiable/ identifying	

6.

		Make sentences to demonstrate your understanding of the differences in usage
Noun	imitation	
Verb	imitate	
Adjective	imitative	

7.

		Make sentences to demonstrate your understanding of the differences in usage
Noun	impress	
Verb	impression	
Adjective	impressive	

8.

		Make sentences to demonstrate your understanding of the differences in usage
Noun	include	
Verb	inclusion	
Adjective	inclusive	

9.

		Make sentences to demonstrate your understanding of the differences in usage
Noun	indication	
Verb	indicate	
Adjective	indicative	

10.

		Make sentences to demonstrate your understanding of the differences in usage
Noun	information	
Verb	inform	
Adjective	informative	

11.

		Make sentences to demonstrate your understanding of the differences in usage
Noun	habitat	
Verb	inhabit	
Adjective	inhabitant/ habitable	

12.

		Make sentences to demonstrate your understanding of the differences in usage
Noun	injury	
Verb	injure	
Adjective	injurious	

13.

		Make sentences to demonstrate your understanding of the differences in usage
Noun	inquiry	
Verb	inquire	
Adjective	inquiring	

14.

		Make sentences to demonstrate your understanding of the differences in usage
Noun	disclosure	
Verb	disclose	
Adjective	disclosed	

14.

		Make sentences to demonstrate your understanding of the differences in usage
Noun	procurement	
Verb	procure	
Adjective	procured	

STEP 43

Even More Prepositional Phrases

Phrase	My sentence
dream of	
excel in	
escape from	
dream about	
excuse for	
be exhausted from	
be exposed to	
be dressed in	
be faithful to	
be familiar with	
fight for	
excel at	
be grateful to	
be gone from	
be furnished with	

Phrase	My sentence
be engaged in	
be filled with	
be finished with	
be fond of	
be envious of	
forget about	
forgive for	
be friendly to	
be engaged to	
be friendly with	
be frightened of	
be equipped with	
be frightened by	
under fire over	
investigation into	
allied with	
prevented from	
jailed for	

STEP 44

Suffixes - #1

As with prefixes, you can expand your vocabulary by learning about suffixes. Knowing a wide range of suffixes can also help you guess the meanings of certain words. Here are some examples:

Suffix	**-ability / -ibility**
Function	quality of being able, having to be something, transforms an adjective into a noun
Example(s)	dependable -> dependability
	sensibility, probability, responsibility, accessibility

Suffix	**-able**
Function	forms adjectives, able to be
Examples	dependable, reliable, insatiable, liable, predictable, payable, calculable, taxable, fashionable, comfortable

Suffix	**-ation, -ication, -sion, -tion**
Function	form nouns that indicate state or process, refers to an action or an instance of an action
Examples	asphyxiation, emancipation, liberation, indication, protection, hesitation, plantation,

Suffix	**-fold**
Function	combines with numbers to form adverbs that indicate how many times something has increased
Examples	twofold, fivefold, tenfold

Suffix / Meaning	Example words	Find the Meanings
-able, -ible, -ble able to	edible	
	audible	
	breakable	
	visible	
	readable	

Suffix / Meaning	Example words	Find the meanings
-acious having the quality of	delicious	
	audacious	
	atrocious	
	conscious	
	precious	

Suffix / Meaning	Example words	Find the Meanings
-al having the quality of, of the kind of, pertaining to, having the form of	functional	
	comical	
	recital	
	renewal	
	rebuttal	

Suffix / Meaning	Example words	Find the Meanings
-ance the act of, a state of being	alliance	
	appearance	
	relevance	
	circumstance	
	grievance	

Make a sentences with each of the following words:

1. bearable

2. forgettable

3. inflatable

4. advisable

5. regrettable

6. debatable

7. accessible

8. collapsible

9. suitable

10. impartial

11. collateral

12. lackadaisical

13. venial

14. venal

15. conjugal

16. vocal

17. acquittal

18. dismissal

19. resemblance

20. elegance

21. instance

22. distance

23. acceptance

24. importance

25. allowance

26. nuisance

27. mortician

28. statistician

29. beautician

30. fearless

31. helpless

32. threefold

33. inability

34. corrigibility

35. compatibility

36. authorship

37. censorship

38. scholarship

39. ownership

40. ostracism

41. panacea

42. paucity

43. predilection

STEP 45

More Transitive Verbs

Do you remember transitive verbs? They require one or more objects. For example,

> *Kenichi wants ice cream.*
> *We learn Chinese.*

You will notice that in the above, we can ask the question "What?"

> Kenichi wants what? Kenichi wants ice cream.
> We learn what? We learn Chinese.

Use each of the following transitive verbs to make a sentence:

1. brush

2. change

3. blow

4. capture

5. collect

6. break

7. bump

8. accept

9. arrest

10. comfort

11. acknowledge

12. bend

13. aggravate

14. cancel

15. open

16. build

17. chase

18. burn

19. bother

20. admit

21. answer

22. close

23. bite

24. call

25. carry

26. charge

27. clutch

28. catch

29. arrest

30. capture

31. hoist

32. nurse

33. grab

34. keep

35. maintain

36. face

37. admire

38. elongate

STEP 46

Prefixes - #2

Prefixes come in front of word stems to create a distinct word or provide new meaning for the word that is formed.

Review

Make sentences with the following words to demonstrate your understanding of them. If by chance you have forgotten the meaning of the prefix and the words below, take the time to review their meanings.

1. Adore

2. Adorn

3. Addict

4. Adhesive

5. Co-pay

6. Undo

Prefix / Meaning	Example words	Find the Meanings
circum-, cir- around, go round, about	circle	
	circumference	
	circumnavigate	
	circuit	
	circumambulate	

Prefix / Meaning	Example words	Find the meanings
com-, con-, co-, col- with, together	colleague	
	coworker	
	co-ed	
	collect	
	cooperate	

Prefix / Meaning	Example words	Find the Meanings
de- away from, down, the opposite of	decline	
	deter	
	depart	
	deescalate	
	desensitize	

Prefix / Meaning	Example words	Find the Meanings
dis-, dif-, di- apart	different	
	dissent	
	dislike	
	distend	
	dishonest	

Prefix / Meaning	Example words	Find the Meanings
pro- forward, going ahead of, supporting	promote	
	proceed	
	protrude	
	promontory	
	propeace	

Prefix / Meaning	Example words	Find the meanings
re- again, back	remember	
	recall	
	reiterate	
	recite	
	rehearse	

Prefix / Meaning	Example words	Find the Meanings
se- apart	seclude	
	secede	
	sedition	
	separate	
	select	

Prefix / Meaning	Example words	Find the Meanings
sub- under, less than	subway	
	subliminal	
	subpar	
	submarine	
	subterranean	

Make a sentence with each of the following words:

1. circumspect

2. circumscribe

3. circumlocution

4. circus

5. circular

6. contemporary

7. contradiction

8. congress

9. conglomerate

10. detach

11. decontaminate

12. deviation

13. disuse

14. disarm

15. disavow

16. disrupt

17. discern

18. propel

19. profess

20. propose

21. regain

22. redo

23. reply

24. recoup

25. segregation

26. select

27. subcontractor

28. untouchable

29. unlockable

30. de-emphasize

31. hindsight

32. misguided

33. overreact

34. upgrade

35. offset

36. disconnect

STEP 47

Numbers Plus

When you hear the word "score," what comes to mind? Soccer? If you first thought about scoring goals in connection with the word "score," you are probably like most people. But score has another meaning - the number, 20.

You might be already familiar with dozen, as representing the number 12.

Here are a few others.

Baker's dozen = 13

Gross = 144

Myriad = 10,000

Googol = 10^1

The word, myriad, means 10,000 but it is also often used to simply mean "a lot."

Myriads of refugees are trying to make their way into Europe.

Imperial System versus Metric System

The metric system is used by almost every country in the world. The United States is one of the few countries that continues to adhere to the imperial system. In fact, the US has agreed to use the metric system as an official system of measurement, but the country has not fully adopted it.

Below are some number-related words that you might find useful to know.

Lengths

12 inches	=	1 foot
3 feet	=	1 yard
3 miles	=	1 league (a league is a rough measurement often used for sea measurements and is sometimes considered anywhere between 3 miles and 8 miles).

Area

1 acre =   43, 500 square feet

Liquid Measurements

Pint   = one eighth of a gallon   = 0.568 litre (UK); 0.473 litre (USA)
Quart   = a quarter of a gallon   = 2 pints   = 1.13 litre (UK); 0.94 litre (US)
Gallon   = four quarts

Metric - Distance

1 kilometer = 1,000 meters
1 kilometer = 100,000 centimeters
1 kilometer = 1,00,000 millimeters

Measurements: From Large to Small

1 centimeter = 10 milliimeters
1 meter = 100 centimeters
1 meter = 1,000 millimeters
1 kilometer = 1,000 meters

Temperature

100 degrees Celsius =
212 degrees Fahrenheit

Word	Abbreviation
kilogram	kg
kilometer	km
centimeter	cm
milligram	mg
millimeter	mm

Write the following figures in words.

1. 21

2. 207

3. 375

4. 972

5. 1,009

6. 1,677

7. 10,332

8. 121,763

9. 339,986

10. 3,998,112

11. 7,934,003

12. 12,995,567

13. 21,777,645,890

14. 106 °F

15. 97 °C

16. 9:30 a.m.

17. 70 kg

18. 20 ml

STEP 48
Suffixes - #2

We continue with the expansion of our knowledge of suffixes.

Suffix   -ify
Function   used to indicate making something/someone different
Example   notify, simplify, identify

Suffix   -ish
Function   to indicate that someone has a certain quality, but to a limite example
Examples   childish, smallish, reddish

Suffix   -ess   / plural -esses
Function   signals female
Examples   hostess, waitress, goddess, lioness, princess, duchess

Suffix   -en
Function   transform, cause to shift to another state
Example   widen, broaden, enlighten

Suffix / Meaning	Example words	Find the Meanings
-ant, -ent, -er, -or one who / inclined to / tending to	applicant	
	supplicant	
	immigrant	
	vigilant	
	brilliant	

Suffix / Meaning	Example words	Find the meanings
-ar, -ary connected with, related to	literary	
	funerary	
	military	
	honorary	
	budgetary	

Suffix / Meaning	Example words	Find the Meanings
-ence quality of, act of	eminence	
	abhorrence	
	dependence	
	excellence	
	negligence	

Suffix / Meaning	Example words	Find the Meanings
-ful full of	grateful	
	helpful	
	mouthful	
	spoonful	
	cheerful	

Suffix / Meaning	Example words	Find the Meanings
-ic, -ac, -il, -ile of, like, pertaining to	analytic	
	imbecile	
	domicile	
	prolific	
	organic	

Suffix / Meaning	Example words	Find the meanings
-ion the act or condition of	culmination	
	celebration	
	corroboration	
	peroration	
	imagination	

Suffix / Meaning	Example words	Find the Meanings
-ism the practice of, support of	communism	
	atheism	
	altruism	
	sexism	
	despotism	

Suffix / Meaning	Example words	Find the Meanings
-ist one who makes, does	artist	
	fabulist	
	linguist	
	pianist	
	flutist	

Make a sentence with each of the following words:

1. outpace

2. outmaneuver

3. outshine

4. outlandish

5. psychology

6. sociology

7. overbook

8. overjoyed

9. overanxiety

10. translator

11 transporter

12. transmit

13. enlighten

14. shepherdess

15. actress

16. embolden

17. christen

18. straighten

19. mistaken

20. frighten

21. awaken

22. threaten

23. chasten

24. hasten

25. clockwise

26. arduous

27. fortitude

28. magnitude

29. quarrelsome

30. cumbersome

31. bibliophile

32. prognosis

STEP 49

Prefixes - #3

Review

Make sentences with the following words to demonstrate your understanding of them.

1. circa

2. circumference

3. combine

4. compare

5. commingle

6. compatriot

7. confound

Prefix / Meaning	Example words	Find the Meanings
epi- upon, on top of	epitaph	
	epilogue	
	epidermis	
	epigram	
	epidermis	

Prefix / Meaning	Example words	Find the meanings
equ-, equi- equal	equidistant	
	equilibrium	
	equalize	
	equitable	
	equanimity	

Prefix / Meaning	Example words	Find the Meanings
ex-, e-, ef- out, from	exit	
	exhale	
	eject	
	exhaust	
	exhale	

Prefix / Meaning	Example words	Find the Meanings
in-, il-, ir-, im-, en- in, into	inject	
	insert	
	immerse	
	instill	
	impose	

Prefix / Meaning	Example words	Find the Meanings
super- over, above, greater	supersonic	
	superwoman	
	superimpose	
	superintendent	
	supermodel	

Prefix / Meaning	Example words	Find the meanings
trans- across	transmit	
	transponder	
	transgender	
	transpose	
	transpire	

Prefix / Meaning	Example words	Find the Meanings
un-, uni- one	unisex	
	uniform	
	unilateral	
	unanimous	
	unidirectional	

Prefix / Meaning	Example words	Find the Meanings
un- not	uncouth	
	uninterested	
	unbalanced	
	unethical	
	unstable	

Make a sentences with each of the following words:

1. telecommuting

2. underestimate

3. undercharge

4. undervalue

5. undermine

6. overestimate

7. overtake

8. feminism

9. sexism

10. Fijian

11. Maltese

12. Swiss

13. Spanish

14. whitish

15. reddish

16. thirtyish

17. childhood

18. adulthood

19. development

20. encouragement

21. solitude

22. physician

23. optician

24. approximately

25. strengthen

26. upgrade

27. undercook

28. unpack

29. semi-retired

30. reconsider

31. prehistoric

32. overrate

STEP 50

Collective Nouns & Group Words - #1

How do you describe a group of birds? What about a group of fish? And still yet, what about a group of politicians? There are English words to take care of each case, and more.

Use each of the following to make a sentence:

1. a school of fish

2. a curriculum of studies

3. a dynasty of kings, queens, or rulers

4. a crew of sailors

5. a council of advisors

6. a constellation of stars

7. a consignment of goods

8. a company of actors

9. a collection of coins

10. a choir of singers

11. a clump of trees

12. a class of students

13. a chain of mountains

14. a chain of events

15. a code of laws

16. a catch of fish (in a net)

17. a cargo of goods

18. a bundle of sticks

19. a bouquet of flowers

20. a board of directors

21. a caravan of travelers

22. a batch of loaves

23. a block of flats

24. a bench of judges

25. a battalion of soldiers

26. a band of musicians

27. a band of robbers

28. a bale of cotton

29. press corps

STEP 51

Verb Tenses - #5

Complete the following table.

Check the meanings of words you do not know.

Verb Tenses			
No.	Verb	Past tense	Past Participle
1	Recast		
2	Recut		
3	Redo		
4	Redraw		
5	Regrind		
6	Regrow		
7	Reknit		
8	Relay		
9	Relearn		
10	Relight		
11	Remake		

Verb Tenses			
No.	Verb	Past tense	Past Participle
12	Rive		
13	Run		
14	Saw		
15	Say		
16	See		
17	Seek		
18	Sell		
19	Send		
20	Set		
21	Sew		
22	Shake		
23	Shave		
24	Shear		
25	Shed		
26	Shine		

Verb Tenses			
No.	Verb	Past tense	Past Participle
27	Shoe		
28	Shoot		
29	Show		
30	Shrink		
31	Shut		
32	Sight-read		
33	Sightsee		
34	Sing		
35	Sink		
36	Skywrite		
37	Slay		
38	Sleep		
39	Slide		
40	Sling		
41	Slink		

No.	Verb	Past tense	Past Participle
42	Rend		
43	Repay		
44	Reread		
45	Rerun		
46	Resell		
47	Resend		
48	Reset		
49	Resew		
50	Reshoot		
51	Resit		
52	Retake		
53	Retell		
54	Retread		
55	Retrofit		
56	Reweave		

No.	Verb	Past tense	Past Participle
57	Rewed		
58	Smite		
59	Snapshot		
60	Sneak		
61	Soothsay		
62	Sow		
63	Speak		
64	Speed		
65	Spell		
66	Spellbind		
67	Spend		
68	Outfly		
69	Outgrow		
70	Outleap		
71	Output		

STEP 52
Word Forms - #10:
Nouns, Verbs, & Adjectives

1.

		Make sentences to demonstrate your understanding of the differences in usage
Noun	insult	
Verb	insult	
Adjective	insulting	

2.

		Make sentences to demonstrate your understanding of the differences in usage
Noun	intention	
Verb	intend	
Adjective	intentional	

3.

		Make sentences to demonstrate your understanding of the differences in usage
Noun	interference	
Verb	interfere	
Adjective	interfering	

4.

		Make sentences to demonstrate your understanding of the differences in usage
Noun	introduction	
Verb	introduce	
Adjective	introductory	

5.

		Make sentences to demonstrate your understanding of the differences in usage
Noun	invention	
Verb	invent	
Adjective	inventive	

6.

		Make sentences to demonstrate your understanding of the differences in usage
Noun	irritation	
Verb	irritate	
Adjective	irritating	

7.

		Make sentences to demonstrate your understanding of the differences in usage
Noun	leadership	
Verb	lead	
Adjective	leading	

8.

		Make sentences to demonstrate your understanding of the differences in usage
Noun	life	
Verb	live	
Adjective	lively/alive	

9.

		Make sentences to demonstrate your understanding of the differences in usage
Noun	refutation	
Verb	refute	
Adjective	refutable	

10.

		Make sentences to demonstrate your understanding of the differences in usage
Noun	statement	
Verb	state	
Adjective	stated	

11.

		Make sentences to demonstrate your understanding of the differences in usage
Noun	loss	
Verb	lose	
Adjective	lost	

12.

		Make sentences to demonstrate your understanding of the differences in usage
Noun	madness	
Verb	madden	
Adjective	mad	

13.

		Make sentences to demonstrate your understanding of the differences in usage
Noun	migration	
Verb	migrate	
Adjective	migratory	

14.

		Make sentences to demonstrate your understanding of the differences in usage
Noun	modernity	
Verb	modernize	
Adjective	modern	

15.

		Make sentences to demonstrate your understanding of the differences in usage
Noun	review	
Verb	review	
Adjective	reviewed	

16.

		Make sentences to demonstrate your understanding of the differences in usage
Noun	requisition	
Verb	requisition	
Adjective	requisite	

17.

		Make sentences to demonstrate your understanding of the differences in usage
Noun	subjugation	
Verb	subjugate	
Adjective	subjugated	

18.

		Make sentences to demonstrate your understanding of the differences in usage
Noun	dissection	
Verb	dissect	
Adjective	dissected/ dissectible	

19.

		Make sentences to demonstrate your understanding of the differences in usage
Noun	block	
Verb	block	
Adjective	blocked	

20.

		Make sentences to demonstrate your understanding of the differences in usage
Noun	despair	
Verb	despair	
Adjective	despairing/ desperate	

21.

		Make sentences to demonstrate your understanding of the differences in usage
Noun	cause	
Verb	cause	
Adjective	causal	

22.

		Make sentences to demonstrate your understanding of the differences in usage
Noun	front	
Verb	front	
Adjective	front/frontal	

23.

		Make sentences to demonstrate your understanding of the differences in usage
Noun	quantification	
Verb	quantify	
Adjective	quantifiable	

24.

		Make sentences to demonstrate your understanding of the differences in usage
Noun	direction	
Verb	direct	
Adjective	direct/ directed	

25.

		Make sentences to demonstrate your understanding of the differences in usage
Noun	employment	
Verb	employ	
Adjective	employable	

26.

		Make sentences to demonstrate your understanding of the differences in usage
Noun	consideration	
Verb	consider	
Adjective	considerable	

27.

		Make sentences to demonstrate your understanding of the differences in usage
Noun	selection	
Verb	select	
Adjective	selective/ selected	

28.

		Make sentences to demonstrate your understanding of the differences in usage
Noun	misconstrual	
Verb	misconstrue	
Adjective	misconstrued	

29.

		Make sentences to demonstrate your understanding of the differences in usage
Noun	transformation	
Verb	transform	
Adjective	transformative	

30.

		Make sentences to demonstrate your understanding of the differences in usage
Noun	stagnation	
Verb	stagnate	
Adjective	stagnant	

31.

		Make sentences to demonstrate your understanding of the differences in usage
Noun	revelation	
Verb	reveal	
Adjective	revealing/ revelatory	

STEP 53

Idiomatic Expressions - #3

(Note that some expressions have both a literal and metaphorical meaning.)

1.

Idiom	breakneck pace
Meaning	
Sample sentence/ My sentence	

2.

Idiom	come down the pike
Meaning	
Sample sentence/ My sentence	

3.

Idiom	have a beef with
Meaning	
Sample sentence/ My sentence	

4.

Idiom	wear (something) on one's sleeve
Meaning	
Sample sentence/ My sentence	

5.

Idiom	pump the brakes
Meaning	
Sample sentence/ My sentence	

6.

Idiom	be caught flat-footed
Meaning	
Sample sentence/ My sentence	

7.

Idiom	trickle down
Meaning	
Sample sentence/ My sentence	

8.

Idiom	set the tone
Meaning	
Sample sentence/ My sentence	

9.

Idiom	be-all and end-all
Meaning	
Sample sentence/ My sentence	

10.

Idiom	take note
Meaning	
Sample sentence/ My sentence	

11.

Idiom	come roaring back
Meaning	
Sample sentence/ My sentence	

12.

Idiom	tamp down
Meaning	
Sample sentence/ My sentence	

13.

Idiom	take on the world
Meaning	
Sample sentence/ My sentence	

14.

Idiom	the other side
Meaning	
Sample sentence/ My sentence	

15.

Idiom	pull for
Meaning	
Sample sentence/ My sentence	

16.

Idiom	a shining example
Meaning	
Sample sentence/ My sentence	

17.

Idiom	household name
Meaning	
Sample sentence/ My sentence	

18.

Idiom	rank and file
Meaning	
Sample sentence/ My sentence	

19.

Idiom	speak off the cuff
Meaning	
Sample sentence/ My sentence	

20.

Idiom	bottom feeder
Meaning	
Sample sentence/ My sentence	

21.

Idiom	buy into (something)
Meaning	
Sample sentence/ My sentence	

22.

Idiom	double down
Meaning	
Sample sentence/ My sentence	

23.

Idiom	put your finger on (something)
Meaning	
Sample sentence/ My sentence	

24.

Idiom	sugarcoat (something)
Meaning	
Sample sentence/ My sentence	

25.

Idiom	think out of the box
Meaning	
Sample sentence/ My sentence	

26.

Idiom	meet (someone) halfway
Meaning	
Sample sentence/ My sentence	

27.

Idiom	cut to the chase
Meaning	
Sample sentence/ My sentence	

28.

Idiom	win-win situation
Meaning	
Sample sentence/ My sentence	

29.

Idiom	screw up
Meaning	
Sample sentence/ My sentence	

30.

Idiom	in the black
Meaning	
Sample sentence/ My sentence	

31.

Idiom	stay on your toes
Meaning	
Sample sentence/ My sentence	

32.

Idiom	get the bugs out
Meaning	
Sample sentence/ My sentence	

33.

Idiom	raise the bar
Meaning	
Sample sentence/ My sentence	

34.

Idiom	a punch to the gut
Meaning	
Sample sentence/ My sentence	

STEP 54

Suffixes - #3

Review

Makes Sentences to Confirm Your Understanding of the Following Words.

1. ageless

2. aimless

3. airless

4. armless

5. blameless

6. bottomless

7. clueless

8. fearless

Suffix / Meaning	Example words	Find the Meanings
-ity, -ty, -y the state of, the character of	infinity	
	diversity	
	ingenuity	
	integrity	
	solidarity	

Suffix / Meaning	Example words	Find the meanings
-ive having the nature of	collective	-
	conclusive	
	inexpensive	
	imperative	
	sedative	

Suffix / Meaning	Example words	Find the Meanings
-less lacking, without	powerless	
	shiftless	
	flawless	
	hopeless	
	artless	

Suffix / Meaning	Example words	Find the Meanings
-logy the study of	seismology	
	cardiology	
	cryptology	
	theology	
	urology	

Suffix / Meaning	Example words	Find the Meanings
-ment the act of	accomplishment	
	augment	
	adjustment	
	amazement	
	amusement	

Suffix / Meaning	Example words	Find the meanings
-ness the quality of	wariness	
	absentmindedness	
	adeptness	
	aggressiveness	
	attractiveness	

Suffix / Meaning	Example words	Find the Meanings
-ory, -ary, -ery having the nature of, a place or thing for	boundary	
	customary	
	visionary	
	secondary	
	contributory	

Suffix / Meaning	Example words	Find the Meanings
-ous, -ose possessing, full of	dangerous	
	ferrous	
	mountainous	
	advantageous	
	ambitious	

Make a sentences with each of the following words:

1. religious

2. arduous

3. cantankerous

4. contemptuous

5. devious

6. disastrous

7. expeditious

8. famous

9. pious

10. copious

11. jealous

12. raucous

13. devious

14. joyous

15. dextrous

16. obvious

17. aqueous

18. onerous

19. bulbous

20. breathless

21. careless

22. faithless

23. groundless

24. hairless

25. harmless

26. greatness

27. baleful

28. sameness

29. rejection

30. partition

31. literally

32. acceptance

STEP 55

Prefixes - #4

Review

Make sentences with the following words:

1. transpire

2. transcend

3. transcribe

4. transfer

5. transform

6. transmit

7. transform

8. translate

Prefix / Meaning	Example words	Find the Meanings
in-, il-, ig-, ir-, im- not	indelible	
	inactive	
	ignoble	
	irrelevant	
	imbalance	

Prefix / Meaning	Example words	Find the meanings
inter- between, among	international	
	intercollege	
	interpose	
	intermingle	
	interfere	

Prefix / Meaning	Example words	Find the Meanings
mal-, male- bad, ill, wrong	malpractice	
	malfunction	
	maleficent	
	malignant	
	maladjust	

Prefix / Meaning	Example words	Find the Meanings
mis- wrong, badly	misjudge	
	mistake	
	mislead	
	misnomer	
	misinterpret	

Prefix / Meaning	Example words	Find the Meanings
act-, ag- to do, to act	activist	
	agent	
	aggressive	
	agree	
	aggrandize	

Prefix / Meaning	Example words	Find the meanings
apert- opening, hole, usually circular phil love	aperture	
	philosopher	
	philology	
	philately	
	philanthropist	

Prefix / Meaning	Example words	Find the Meanings
bas- low	basement	
	bas-relief	
	basic	
	baseless	
	bashful	

Prefix/Affix/Meaning	Example words	Find the Meanings
cap-, capt-, -cip, -cept, -ceive to take, to hold, to seize	capture	
	receive	
	receptacle	
	capsule	
	miniscule	

Make a sentence with each of the following words:

1. impossible

2. irreversible

3. ignorant

4. ignoble

5. illicit

6. illegible

7. irascible

8. illiterate

9. impostor

10. interact

11. interagency

12. intercede

13. interchange

14. interconnection

15. interdependency

16. interdiction

17. interject

18. interlace

19. actionable

20. activate

21. actually

22. capabilities

23. capitalize

24. capture

STEP 56

Still More Prepositional Phrases

Phrase	My sentence
be eligible for	
be grateful for	
be grateful to	
be innocent of	
hope for	
hide from	
be guilty of	
be wary of	
be cognizant of	
be gone from	
be scared of	
in moderation	
in vain	
in no time	

Phrase	My sentence
in two	
in one's free time	
in half	
in other words	
in town	
in pain	
in touch	
in particular	
in time	
in person	
in the news	
in practice	
in theory	
in the mountains	
in prison	
in private	
in public	
in jail	

Phrase	My sentence
in return	
in the mood for	
in (somebody's) interest	
in the meantime	
in somebody's opinion	
in the habit of	
in season	
in the end	
in season	
in the dark	
in self-defense	
in the beginning	
in secret	
in the air	
in tears	
in tatters	
in toto	
in full bloom	

STEP 57

Collective Nouns & Group Words - #2

Use each of the phrases below to make a sentence.

1. a row of chairs

2. a rope of pearls

3. a queue of people

4. a pile of stones

5. a party of friends

6. an anthology of poems

7. an album of photos

8. an army of ants

9. an assembly of members

10. a menagerie of wild animals

11. a litter of puppies (at the same birth)

12. a library of books

13. a lock of hair

14. a legion of soldiers

15. a hoard of jewels

16. a hive of bees

17. a herd of cattle

18. a heap of ruins

19. a grove of trees

20. a group of islands

21. a gang of workmen

22. a gaggle of geese

23. a flotilla of ships

24. a gallery of paintings

25. a forest of trees

26. a flock of sheep

27. a flight of birds

28. a fleet of cars

STEP 58

Prefixes - #5

Review

Use the following words in a sentence.

1. unit

2. unicycle

3. unify

4. unique

5. universal

6. twins

7. triplets

8. quadriplegic

Prefix / Meaning	Example words	Find the Meanings
mono- one, alone, single	monologue	
	monopoly	
	monotone	
	monomania	
	monocle	

Prefix / Meaning	Example words	Find the meanings
non- not, the reverse of	nonentity	
	nonpareil	
	nonprofit	
	nonchalant	
	nondescript	

Prefix / Meaning	Example words	Find the Meanings
ob- in front, towards, against, in front of, in the way of	obvious	
	obstacle	
	obtrude	
	obverse	
	obsolete	

Prefix / Meaning	Example words	Find the Meanings
omni- everywhere	omniscient	
	omnibus	
	omnipresent	
	omnipotent	
	omnicompetent	

Prefix / Meaning	Example words	Find the Meanings
phono- relating to voice or speech	phonology	
	phonograph	
	phonemics	
	phonics	
	phonologist	

Prefix / Meaning	Example words	Find the meanings
cred-, credit- to believe	credit	
	incredible	
	credence	
	credible	
	credulous	

Prefix / Meaning	Example words	Find the Meanings
curr-, curs-, -cours- to run	current	
	currency	
	recourse	
	cursory	
	cursive	

Prefix / Meaning	Example words	Find the Meanings
dic-, dict- to say	diction	
	dictionary	
	dictate	
	indict	
	indicate	

Make a sentence with each of the following words:

1. indict

2. dictate

3. proceed

4. proactive

5. precedence

6. bassinet

7. bastion

8. baste

9. object

10. obligate

11. observant

12. offend

13. obligatory

14. oblivion

15. obvious

16. obdurate

17. obedience

18. optimism

19. object

20. objective

STEP 59
Suffixes - #4

Review

Make sentences with each of the following words:

1. edify

2. vilify

3. codify

4. purify

5. modify

6. solidify

7. mollify

8. prettify

Suffix / Meaning	Example words	Find the Meanings
-some full of, like	lonesome	
	awesome	
	troublesome	
	burdensome	
	handsome	

Suffix / Meaning	Example words	Find the meanings
-tude the state of, the quality of, the ability to	amplitude	
	ingratitude	
	fortitude	
	attitude	
	aptitude	

Suffix / Meaning	Example words	Find the Meanings
-y full of, somewhat, somewhat like	creamy	
	juicy	
	breezy	
	cloudy	
	stormy	

Suffix / Meaning	Example words	Find the Meanings
-arium, -orium place for	emporium	
	crematorium	
	sanatorium	
	aquarium	
	planetarium	

Make a sentence with each of the following words:

1. irksome

2. cumbersome

3. noisome

4. gruesome

5. wholesome

6. troublesome

7. lonesome

8. winsome

9. burdensome

10. loathsome

11. altitude

12. latitude

13. gratitude

14. servitude

15. rectitude

16. solicitude

17. magnitude

18. fortitude

19. desuetude

20. vicissitude

21. fiery

22. slippery

23. nasty

24. misty

25. grumpy

26. moody

27. glossy

28. exemplify

29. utility

30. fraternity

31. impeccable

32. progressive

33. forgetful

34. complication

35. postage

36. payee

37. equality

38. brutality

39. workmanship

STEP 60

Collective Nouns and Group Words - #3

Make a sentence with each of the following phrases.

1. a society of people

2. a set of tools

3. a shower of rain

4. a squad of soldiers

5. a staff of officials

6. a stock of goods

7. a suit of clothes

8. a swarm of bees

9. a team of players

10. a congregation of churchgoers

11. a brood of chickens

12. a litter of cubs

13. a school of dolphins

14. a herd of giraffes

15. a swarm of insects

16. a pride of lions

17. a pod of whales

18. a clutch of biographies

19. a gaggle of reporters

20. a parliament of owls

21. a gaggle of politicians

22. a clutch of microphones

23. a bevy of ladies

24. an archipelago of islands

25. an armada of ships

26. a bunch of grapes

27. a chest of drawers

28. a gam of whales

29. an orchard of fruit trees

30. a hail of bullets

STEP 61

Affixes

Affix is the general word covering both prefixes and suffixes. Some affixes are attached to the beginning of a word while in some other cases they are attached at the end. In other words, they behave as prefixes in some cases and as suffixes in others.

Review / Research : Make a sentence with each of the following words. If you are not sure about the meaning, do some research, and learn the root of the word.

1. podiatry

2. pedal

3. paranormal

4. agriculture

5. pedicure

6. perimeter

Prefix / Meaning	Example words	Find the Meanings
per- through	pervade	
	perspective	
	perceive	
	pertain	
	pertinent	

Prefix / Meaning	Example words	Find the meanings
poly- many	polytechnic	
	polysyllable	
	polymath	
	polymerized	
	polysaturated	

Prefix / Meaning	Example words	Find the Meanings
post- after	postwar	
	postpone	
	postpartum	
	postmortem	
	postmodern	

Prefix / Meaning	Example words	Find the Meanings
pre- before, earlier than	preview	
	prehistoric	
	preceded	
	prevent	
	precocious	

Affix / Meaning	Example words	Find the Meanings
duc-, duct- to lead	conduct	
	conductor	
	aqueduct	
	induce	
	induction	

Prefix / Meaning	Example words	Find the meanings
equ- equal	equanimity	
	equable	
	equality	
	equity	
	equidistant	

Prefix / Meaning	Example words	Find the Meanings
fac-, fact-, fic-, fect- to make, to do	factory	
	factotum	
	facility	
	fiction	
	affect	

Affix / Meaning	Example words	Find the Meanings
fer-, ferr- to carry, to bring	infer	
	defer	
	ferry	
	refer	
	prefer	

Make a sentences with each of the following words:

1. behavior

2. flank

3. astride

4. beseech

5. factional

6. factoid

7. factory

8. fracture

9. cogent

10. robust

11. apparent

12. applaud

13. appreciate

14. applet

15. episode

16. supernatural

17. creator

18. horror

19. experimental

20. progressive

21. ward

STEP 62

Idiomatic Expressions - #4

(Note that some expressions have both a literal and metaphorical meaning.)

1.

Idiom	open-minded
Meaning	
Sample sentence/ My sentence	

2.

Idiom	on a roll
Meaning	
Sample sentence/ My sentence	

3.

Idiom	get something off your chest
Meaning	
Sample sentence/ My sentence	

4.

Idiom	plant a seed
Meaning	
Sample sentence/ My sentence	

5.

Idiom	a bitter pill to swallow
Meaning	
Sample sentence/ My sentence	

6.

Idiom	wouldn't be caught dead
Meaning	
Sample sentence/ My sentence	

7.

Idiom	speak truth to power
Meaning	
Sample sentence/ My sentence	

8.

Idiom	close the door on
Meaning	
Sample sentence/ My sentence	

9.

Idiom	sting of defeat
Meaning	
Sample sentence/ My sentence	

10.

Idiom	press on
Meaning	
Sample sentence/ My sentence	

11.

Idiom	go off
Meaning	
Sample sentence/ My sentence	

12.

Idiom	beg the question
Meaning	
Sample sentence/ My sentence	

13.

Idiom	skyrocket
Meaning	
Sample sentence/ My sentence	

14.

Idiom	come to fruition
Meaning	
Sample sentence/ My sentence	

15.

Idiom	in shambles
Meaning	
Sample sentence/ My sentence	

16.

Idiom	it'll never fly
Meaning	
Sample sentence/ My sentence	

17.

Idiom	jog someone's memory
Meaning	
Sample sentence/ My sentence	

18.

Idiom	keep a tight rein on
Meaning	
Sample sentence/ My sentence	

19.

Idiom	a knee-jerk reaction
Meaning	
Sample sentence/ My sentence	

20.

Idiom	lame duck
Meaning	
Sample sentence/ My sentence	

21.

Idiom	a late bloomer
Meaning	
Sample sentence/ My sentence	

22.

Idiom	lay someone to rest
Meaning	
Sample sentence/ My sentence	

23.

Idiom	let one's hair down
Meaning	
Sample sentence/ My sentence	

24.

Idiom	leave well enough alone
Meaning	
Sample sentence/ My sentence	

STEP 63

The Subjunctive

One of the most troublesome grammar points is the subjunctive. In normal use, you learn that when you use the third person singular (he, she, it), you add 's' or 'es' to the verb. For example,

He **goes** to school at 9 a.m. every weekday.

The subjunctive is usually used for situations that have not yet come to pass. They may also be used for situations that are merely hypothetical, not real. Further, they may be used to express a person's imagination, hopes, expectations, or demands.

Subjunctive "That Clauses"

In subjunctive use, however, you use the basic form of the verb (do, go, be, eat, say, tell, sweep, stand, etc.) even for third-person singular constructions.

The form: that + the subject + the simple form of the verb

For example,
> Kenichi insisted that Lorraine **go** alone to the party.
> I recommended that he not **do** that magic trick.
> It is important that she **be** aware of her surroundings at all times.
> It is important that you **be** the leader that you say you want.
> The parents insist that each of their children **get** enough sleep every night.
> It is important that she **be** told the importance of her art.

When it comes to this form of the subjunctive, there are particular words, phrases, and clauses (some involving verbs and others involving nouns or adjectives) that can trigger the use of the simple verb form.

You may have noticed the following in the sentences above:

    ...insisted that...
    ...important that...

When you see the following verbs in "that-clauses" it is a signal that you need to use a subjective. Because many people are not familiar with the subjunctive when they come across it in a test, it looks strange and so they assume it cannot be correct. So, get to know more about the subjunctive.

Verbs
- demand that
    - He demanded that the company **pay** him immediately.
- recommend that
- suggest that

Nouns/Adjectives

• essential	• important	• insistence	• proposal
• requirement	• stipulation	• proviso	• urge

Be careful about sentences that use the above words. Scrutinize them. They may be a subjunctive construction lying in wait to trap you.

Make a sentence with each of the following phrases:

1) it is vital (that)

2) it is important (that)

3) it is critical (that)

4) request (that)

5) propose (that)

6) demand (that)

7) advise (that)

8) ask (that)

9) insist (that)

10) there is a stipulation (that)

11) there is a proviso (that)

12) recommend (that)

13) suggest (that)

14) it is essential (that)

STEP 64
Words & Their Connections

When you see the word, "avian," what comes to mind? Birds? And when you see the word, "piscine," what comes to mind? Fish? Still more, when you see the word "equine," do you make the connection between this word and horses?

Knowing what certain words pertain to can unlock a whole lot of meaning for you as an English speaker and communicator.

It goes without saying that if you are not sure how to use a word in a sentence, search for its meaning in the dictionary.

Some dictionaries provide sample sentences. But, after you have understood the meaning, you should still try to use the word by yourself. This will strengthen your own connection to the word. And we know that the more often you use a word, the greater the chances that you will retain the meaning of that word.

For example, the word porcine relates to pigs, while vitrine relates to glass display cases. So, whenever you see any of these words appear in a phrase, you can deduce what they are all about.

WORD:	pertains to ...
astral	stars
astronomical	the scientific study of stars and planets
celestial	sky, heaven, space
cosmic	planets, stars, space, universse
extraterrestrial	things existing on planets other than Earth
galactic	a galaxy
heavenly	sky, moon, stars, etc.
intergalactic	happening between different galaxies, for example, travel
interplanetary	happening between different planets, for example, travel
interstellar	between the stars
Martian	Mars (the planet)
meteoric	meteors
sidereal	stars
solar	sun
stellar	stars
amphibious	capable of living in both water and on land
androgynous	animal or plant that has both male and female parts
anthropoid	like human
aquatic	growing in water, living in water, or living or growing near water
arboreal	living trees
asexual	a creature with no sex organs
caged	kept inside a cage
captive	kept in a zoo, park, or natural environment (for example, animal)
cold-blooded	animals whose body temperature changes according to the environment
diurnal	awake and active during the day
domestic	animal kept as a pet or on farm
domesticated	animal trained to live with humans or work for humans
downy	covered in small hairs or feathers (soft)
draught	animal used to pull heavy things
extinct	no longer exists
feathered	covered with feathers / made from feathers
feral	wild
fluffy	covered with soft hairs or feathers (soft)

Exercise: Form a sentence with each of the following.

1. stellar

2. feral

3. celestial

4. arboreal

5. amphibious

6. galactic

7. solar

8. lunar

9. heavenly

10. aquatic

11. botanic

12. corporeal

13. aquatic

14. aerial

15. crustacean

WORD:	pertains to ...
flying	a creature that is able to fly
freshwater	water that does not have salt
furred	covered either with fur or something that looks like fur
furry	covered with fur
giant	an animal or plant name that is larger than other similar animals or plants
gregarious	animals living in groups
horned	an animal that has horns
house-trained	a pet that has been trained to go to "toilet" outside or in a special place (both urine and feces)
house-broken	a pet that has been trained to go to "toilet" outside or in a special place (both urine and feces)
indigenous	animals or plants that are known to have developed in a particular place
juvenile	young animals or plants
lop-eared	an animal with long ears hanging by the sides of the head
man-eating	an animal that kills and eats human beings
mangy	an animal with the disease, mange; involves itchy skin and loss of fur
mature	an animal or plant that has grown to its full size
migratory	a bird or animal that moves from one place to another at some time of the year
native	a place where an animal or plant belongs or has always been
naturalized	a plant or animal that has survived in a place but was actually brought from somewhere else initially
nocturnal	animals that are active at night
omnivorous	animals that eat both plants and meat
parasitic	a plant or animal that lives in or on another type of plant or animal
pedigree	an animal of a particular breed whose family history has been recorded for several generations

Exercise: Form a sentence with each of the following.

1. nocturnal

2. herbivorous

3. carnivorous

4. furry

5. gregarious

6. migratory

7. predatory

8. mammalian

9. spineless

10. prey

11. aggressive

12. timid

13. assertive

14. miniature

15. juvenile

WORD:	pertains to ...
petrified	a plant or animal that died some time ago and whose body has turned into rock
pigmy / pigmy	an animal, person, or plant that is unusually small in size
poisonous	anything that is capable of producing poison
polymorphous	a plant or animal that has different forms at different stages of its development
predatory	animals that kill and eat other animals
purebred	an animal that comes from parents of the same breed
rabid	an animal that has rabies (disease)
rogue	an animal that lives separately from others and is considered dangerous
saltwater	living in the sea or in water that has salt in it
savage	a very dangerous animal
scaly	an animal that has scales on the skin, for example, a snake
shy	an animal that tries to keep away from people by hiding
simian	connected or similar to an ape or a monkey
social	animals that live in groups
spineless	animals that have no spine
stuffed	an animal that is dead and has its body filled to make it look as though it were alive
tame	an animal that has been trained to get used to being around people
temperate	plants and animals that live in temperate parts of the world
territorial	animals or people that are eager to protect the area in which they live; they might get aggressive or hurt animals or people who intrude on their territory
tolerant	plants or animals that are tolerant of particular conditions are able to survive in those conditions where other animals or plants might not be able to survive
transgenic	a plant or animal that has genes from another plant or animal through the use of a special laboratory technique

Exercise: Form a sentence with each of the following.

1. temperate

2. predatory

3. savage

4. rabid

5. poisonous

6. social

7. stationery

8. tolerant

9. reptilian

10. antagonist

11. protagonist

12. vicious

13. virtuous

14. liminal

15. reservoir

STEP 65
Word Forms - #11: Nouns, Verbs, & Adjectives

1.

		Make sentences to demonstrate your understanding of the differences in usage
Noun	seduction	
Verb	seduce	
Adjective	seductive	

2.

		Make sentences to demonstrate your understanding of the differences in usage
Noun	move	
Verb	move	
Adjective	movable	

3.

		Make sentences to demonstrate your understanding of the differences in usage
Noun	narrowness	
Verb	narrow	
Adjective	narrow	

4.

		Make sentences to demonstrate your understanding of the differences in usage
Noun	nationality	
Verb	nationalize	
Adjective	national	

5.

		Make sentences to demonstrate your understanding of the differences in usage
Noun	ownership	
Verb	own	
Adjective	own	

6.

		Make sentences to demonstrate your understanding of the differences in usage
Noun	performance	
Verb	perform	
Adjective	performing	

7.

		Make sentences to demonstrate your understanding of the differences in usage
Noun	persuasion	
Verb	persuade	
Adjective	persuasive	

8.

		Make sentences to demonstrate your understanding of the differences in usage
Noun	pleasure	
Verb	please	
Adjective	pleasant	

9.

		Make sentences to demonstrate your understanding of the differences in usage
Noun	popularity	
Verb	popularize	
Adjective	popular	

10.

		Make sentences to demonstrate your understanding of the differences in usage
Noun	quickness	
Verb	quicken	
Adjective	quick	

11.

		Make sentences to demonstrate your understanding of the differences in usage
Noun	redness	
Verb	redden	
Adjective	red	

12.

		Make sentences to demonstrate your understanding of the differences in usage
Noun	sadness	
Verb	sadden	
Adjective	sad	

13.

		Make sentences to demonstrate your understanding of the differences in usage
Noun	security	
Verb	secure	
Adjective	secure	

14.

		Make sentences to demonstrate your understanding of the differences in usage
Noun	sight	
Verb	see	
Adjective	sighted	

15.

		Make sentences to demonstrate your understanding of the differences in usage
Noun	entrenchment	
Verb	entrench	
Adjective	entrenched	

STEP 66
Adjectives - #1:
The Comparative & Superlative

You are good at playing soccer. Or was it handball? Your best friend, however, is better at both games. And that guy or gal that you never seem to get along with somehow is the best at both games.

You are good.	**Adjective**
Your best friend is better.	**Comparative** (comparing two things)
That other person is the best.	**Superlative** (comparing three or more things)

One-syllable Adjectives

Most one-syllable adjectives add -er for the comparative and -est for the superlative. Here are some examples.

Positive	Comparative	Superlative
rich	richer	the richest
cool	cooler	the coolest
calm	calmer	the calmest
bright	brighter	the brightest
sweet	sweeter	the sweetest

Exceptions

It is dangerous to rely only on rules to learn English because there are always exceptions to every rule. Even though most one-syllable words use -er for the comparative and -est for the superlative, sometimes, this is not the case. You will see cases where more is attached to the verb for the comparative and the most is attached to the adjective for the superlative.

Here are some examples:

> The new software is making animation look **more real.**
>
> I used to think my mother was always wrong but the older I get the **more right** she is.
>
> Sometimes we do the wrong thing with **the most wrong** timing.
>
> As he grew even **more ill**, he became determined to finish the book he had begun.
>
> I've become **more loath** to go to bed early.
>
> It's **more fun** to eat with friends than to dine alone.
>
> Flying a plane was certainly **the most fun** I had had in a long time.
>
> This is certainly **more dull** than I had ever imagined.
>
> This is **duller** than I had ever imagined. (Also all right)

Adjectives Formed from Past Participles

We do not add -er or -est to adjectives formed from past participles when making comparisons.

An excited puppy	A more excited puppy	The most excited puppy
A lost bird	A more lost bird	The most lost bird
A disgusted student	A more disgusted student	The most disgusted student
A frightened father	A more frightened father	The most frightened father

Two-syllable Adjectives

Positive	Comparative	Superlative
pretty	prettier	prettiest
happy	happier	happiest
easy	easier	easiest
dirty	dirtier	dirtiest
simple	simpler	simplest
narrow	narrower	narrowest
clever	cleverer	cleverest

Many two-syllable adjectives can also be formed using more for the comparative and the most for the superlative. Here are some examples.

More money does not necessarily make us more happy.
Some of the participants in the show are more pretty than talented.
She is more clever than I thought.
It might be more easy to do the work yourself than to wait for someone else to do it.

Three-syllable Adjectives

Positive	Comparative	Superlative
glorious	more glorious	the most glorious
delightful	more delightful	the most delightful
fanciful	more fanciful	the most fanciful
beautiful	more beautiful	the most beautiful
positive	more positive	the most positive
charming	more charming	the most charming

Irregular Forms

Good	Better	Best
Bad	Worse	Worst
Far (physical distance)	Farther (than)	The farthest
Far (additional, more advanced)	Further (than)	The furthest

Make a sentence with each of the following phrases.

1. more thrilling

2. more frightening

3. the most exhausting

4. the most annoying

5. more embarrassing

6. a good deal heavier

7. far older than

8. far more understanding than

9. a bit older than

10. slightly taller than

11. the highest

12. longer than

13. nearly as high as

14. the most convincing

15. the more benign

16. a far greater threat

17. the most talented

18. flatter than

19. a bit less

20. so much more

21. far less concerned

STEP 67
Even More Transitive Verbs

You remember transitive verbs, don't you? They are verbs that usually requre a direct object, for example, "I own <u>the building</u>" or "Parents bring up <u>their children</u> to be good citizens." Note that some verbs are both transitive and intransitive, meaning that they can be used in other patterns where there is no direct object. For example, "She teaches children" is transitive whereas in, "She teaches without seeming to do so," teach is intransitive.

Make a sentence with each of the following transitive verbs:

1. move

2. murder

3. name

4. nurse

5. munch

6. order

7. open

8. mock

9. number

10. lower

11. make

12. maintain

13. love

14. massage

15. notice

16. offend

17. marry

18. mark

19. melt

20. kill

21. link

22. lighten

23. lose

24. lick

25. load

26. lock

27. mix

28. list

29. limit

30. light

31. lag

32. knock

33. lay

34. lead

35. lift

36. leave

37. lean

38. let

39. hoist

40. hurt

41. examine

42. fascinate

43. daze

44. escort

45. hurry

46. deceive

47. encircle

48. honour

49. dazzle

50. injure

STEP 68

More Prefixes & Suffixes

Review / Research : Make sentences

1. martyrdom

2. boredom

3. wisdom

4. kingdom

5. overrun

6. seldom

7. architecture

8. archway

9. enclave

10. archaeology

11. archbishop

12. archenemy

13. unable

14. impossible

15. demotivate

16. extraordinary

17. insecure

18. interactive

19. rewrite

Suffix / Meaning	Example words	Find the Meanings
-graph to write	monograph	
	epigraph	
	graphology	
	sonograph	
	photograph	

Suffix / Meaning	Example words	Find the meanings
-mit, -mis to send	admit	
	hermit	
	submit	
	vomit	
	remit	

Suffix/Affix/Meaning	Example words	Find the Meanings
-scrib, script- to write	inscribe	
	describe	
	subscribe	
	scripture	
	scribble	

Suffix / Meaning	Example words	Find the Meanings
-iferous producing, bearing, yielding	aquiferous	
	vociferous	
	coniferous	
	luciferous	
	carboniferous	

Affix / Meaning	Example words	Find the Meanings
-sta, stat-, -sist, -stit-, -sist to stand, to make stand	constant	
	consist	
	constable	
	statistics	
	statute	

Prefix / Meaning	Example words	Find the meanings
tact- to touch	contact	
	tactile	
	intact	
	tactical	
	tactful	

Affix / Meaning	Example words	Find the Meanings
ten-, tent-, -tain to hold	contain	
	retain	
	tenure	
	tenuous	
	tentative	

Prefix/Affix/Meaning	Example words	Find the Meanings
tend-, tens-, tent- to stretch	tension	
	extend	
	distend	
	tendentious	
	contend	

Prefix / Meaning	Example words	Find the Meanings
tract- to drag, to draw	attract	
	retract	
	subtract	
	contract	
	extract	

Prefix/Affix/Meaning	Example words	Find the meanings
-ven, -vent to come	convene	
	advent	
	intervene	
	subvention	
	convention	

Prefix / Meaning	Example words	Find the Meanings
-ver, -vert, -vers to turn	avert	
	reverse	
	reverse	
	subvert	
	revert	

Prefix / Meaning	Example words	Find the Meanings
intra- inside, within, interior, during	intrastate	
	intrapreneur	
	intranet	
	intractable	
	intramural	

Make a sentence with each of the following words:

1. unhappiness

2. unemployed

3. untested

4. discontented

5. interactive

6. aeroplanes

7. aeronautics

8. aftermath

9. astrophysics

10. automatic

11. automobile

12. autonomous

13. cardiologist

14. cardiogram

15. cryptocurrency

16. cryptic

17. divest

18. invest

19. ecology

20. economy

21. exhale

22. exile

23. exit

24. geopolitical

STEP 69

Articles: A, An, The

Many English learners readily admit that the use of articles (a, an, the) can be a pain. This is probably the case because in some languages there are no articles to worry about.

Let's begin with a / an and their use with some types of nouns.

Use a / an with Singular Countable Nouns
- a basket
- a pen
- a basketball
- an iPhone
- an apple
- a brochure

Use the with Singular Countable Nouns
- the basket
- the pen
- the basketball
- the iPhone
- the apple
- the brochure
- the plug
- the orange
- the table
- the apricot

Use the with `Plural Countable Nouns

- the baskets
- the pens
- the basketballs
- the iPhones
- the apples
- the brochures
- the plugs
- the oranges
- the tables
- the apricots

Don't use a / an before Uncountable Nouns

My favorite food is rice.

We need fresh air in this room.

My grandmother always gives me good advice.

In my business, I accept cash.

You need determination to achieve your goals.

Use the before Uncountable Nouns when Focusing on Something Specific

- The rice in this bag is rotten.
- The air in this hall is stale.
- The advice my grandmother gave me yesterday was pretty good.
- The cash that she put on the table was not enough.
- You need the determination of a tiger if you want to achieve your goals.

Making Uncountable Nouns Countable

You can use quantity expressions such as the following:

- She handed me **a piece of** gum.
- We saw **bits of** debris floating on the water.
- Each family got **two bags of** rice for the winter.
- You need at least **three bars of** soap to bathe a baby elephant.
- Is it good to drink **a cup of** milk for breakfast?
- Some say that **a bottle of** beer a day keeps the doctor away.
- That restaurant sells a fabulous **bowl of** clam chowder.
- It is not bad to have **a little** rain every now and then.
- There isn't **any** water left in the well.
- There is **no** gas in the tank.
- He has **some** dignity left, I hope.
- He has **a lot of** money, but so does she.
- We can arrive in **plenty of** time.
- We spent **most of** the time complaining about the weather.

In General Terms

- **Books** are good companions.
- **Philosophy** encourages one to think.
- **Water** is necessary for life.
- **Heroes** die young.
- **Children** should be both heard and seen.
- **Money** talks.
- **Music** is the language of love.

In all the above cases, we are talking about the item in question <u>in general</u> terms, not focusing on a specific instance of it. In that case, there is no need to use "**the**."

In Specific Terms

When you want to refer to a specific item that the listener or reader also know about, you can use the.

- **The books** in my library are good companions.
- **The philosophy** that guides your thinking is pretty impressive.
- **The water** in this bottle is hot.
- **The boys** in the choir really know how to raise the roof.
- **The hero** in this movie really tried to help as many people as possible.
- **The children** in our local club are all very hardworking.
- I have used up all **the money** I saved for my college education.
- **The music** of Chopin is definitely my favorite.

You may use the when talking about some Inventions

- **The television** was invented in the United States.
- **The computer** is a marvelous tool.

As above, when speaking about a specific invention or specific inventions, you can use '**the**.'

- The televisions in the building are all dead.

You may use 'the' when talking about musical instruments

- I play the piano.
- She plays the guitar.
- They both play the flute.
- I have been playing the violin for fifteen years.

'

But,

I play piano in a musical group.

I used to play flute in the Boston Symphony Orchestra.

Determiners

These include words such as the following:

the, my, this, some, each, every, any

Articles:

a/an, then

Demonstratives:

this, that, these, those

Possessives:

my, your, his, her, its, our , their, John's, Mr Robson's, Mrs. Marria's

Quantifiers:

a few, few, fewer, a little, little, many, much, more, most, some, any

Numbers:

one, two, three, four, five, etc.

You may not use an article before determiners

I love my puppy. [NOT: I love ~~the~~ my puppy]

The: Things in the Physical Environment
- the sun
- the moon
- the stars
- the earth
- the planet
- the grass
- the forest
- the jungle
- the sea
- the ocean

The: Everyday Things; Not Necessarily Specific

I am going to the bank. (it does not matter which bank)

I am going to take the train. (it does not matter which train)

I am going to the clinic. (it does not matter which clinic)

Let's search **the Internet.**

If you hear it on **the radio**, you better believe it

That story in **the newspaper** is fake.

But,

I don't like watching television. [NOT the television]

A / An : When Talking about Jobs

She's an architect.

He's a sculptor.

She's a bartender.

He's a stonemason.

The definite article goes in front of some geographical names - not all.

Do not use the before the names of countries and territories.

We flew to Hong Kong in the morning.

I have never been to Croatia.

You must visit Australia.

Some countries, however, take the as part of their names. These are mostly countries that are a group.

the Bahamas	the Cayman Islands	the Central African Republic	the Channel Islands
the Comoros	the Czech Republic	the Dominican Republic	the Falkland Islands
the Gambia	the Isle of Man	the Ivory Coast	the Maldives
the Marshall Islands	the Netherlands	the Netherlands Antilles	the Philippines
the Solomon Islands	the Turks and Caicos Islands	the United Arab Emirates	the United Kingdom
the United States			

You may not use <u>the</u> before the names of:

Lakes:	Lake Geneva, Lake Chad, Lake Victoria, Lake Volta, Oguta Lake, Basalt Lake
States:	Arizona, Massachusetts, Vermont, California, Washington, Maine
Streets:	Penny Street, Orchard Street, Wilshire Street
Islands:	Java, Hainan, Jamaica, Bhola Island, Batam, South Island
Continents:	Africa, Asia, Europe, North America, South America, Australia
Mountains:	Mount Everest, Mount Fuji, Mount McKinley, Mount Kilmanjaro

You may use <u>the</u> for some places

Mountain ranges:	the Alps, the Andes, the Appalachians, the Atlas Mountains, the Caucasus, the Himalayas, the Pyrenees, the Rockies (the Rocky Mountains), the Urals

You may use 'the' before the names of:

Rivers: the Amazon, the Colorado, the Columbia, the Danube, the Don, the Euphrates, the Ganges, the Huang, the Hudson, the Indus, the Jordan, the Lena, the Mackenzie, the Mekong, the Mississippi, the Missouri, the Niger, the Nile, the Ohio, the Orinoco, the Po, the Rhine, the Rhone, the Rio Grande, the St. Lawrence, the Seine, the Thames, the Tiber, the Tigris, the Volga, the Yangtze

Deserts: The Sahara desert, the Mojave Desert

Seas: the Adriatic Sea, the Aegean Sea, the Arabian Sea, the Arctic Ocean, the Atlantic (Ocean), the Baltic (Sea), the Black Sea, the Caribbean (Sea), the Caspian (Sea), the Coral Sea, the Gulf of Aden, the Gulf of Mexico, the Gulf of Oman

Geographical Regions/Other Features:
the equator, the Far East, the Gobi (desert), the Kalahari (desert), the Middle East, the Near East, the North Pole, the Occident, the Orient, the Panama Canal, the Sahara (desert), the South Pole, the Suez Canal, the Tropic of Cancer, the Tropic of Capricorn

Use of <u>the</u> to describe groups

You may use the definite article to describe groups:

the rich	=	rich people
the blind	=	blind people
the poor	=	poor people
the gifted	=	gifted people
the homeless	=	homeless people

Use of 'the' with Dates

For months (don't use the):

My birthday is in June.

We will launch the project in January.

Our reunion is in December.

Specific Date

Use <u>the</u> when speaking, as below:

> Let's get together on **the** 5th of June.

Do not use <u>the</u> when writing, as below:

> Let's get together on 5th June.

Seasons (informal)

> In the summer, I love to go to hot springs.
>
> We don't see that many birds here in the fall.

Seasons (formal)

> In summer, many birds gather in southern Japan.

Specific Season (Use the)

> That was the winter of my discontent.
>
> The winter around here is unbearable.

Building versus Activity

> We are going to be at the school this afternoon.
> (focus on the building)
>
> He has been sent to the hospital. (focus on the building)
> We are going to be in school this afternoon.
> (focus on learning activity)
>
> My friend has been in hospital for the past three weeks.
> (focus on being a patient)

Go to Bed

> I go to bed at 9 o'clock. [NOT: I go to the bed...]

Go to Work

> I go to work at 9 a.m. [NOT: I go to the work...]

Make a sentence with each of the following verbs:

1. pounce

2. replace

3. emerge

4. raise

5. unload

6. weigh

7. sigh

8. sign

9. burst

10. fortify

11. fetch

12. grasp

13. shelter

14. sweep

15. hinge

16. seat

17. peek

18. widen

19. design

20. combine

21. relocate

22. insert

23. unbolt

24. harvest

25. bulldoze

26. glide

27. scamper

28. flee

29. rummage

30. reenter

31. relay

32. sprawl

33. freeze

34. suspend

35. fling

36. chain

37. tilt

38. circle

39. bend

40. linger

41. sneak

42. tramp

43. perch

44. mull

45. stare

46. regard

47. scrutinize

48. survey

49. view

50. clean

51. clear

52. view

53. bathe

54. tickle

55. raise

56. shoot

57. puzzle

58. question

59. swallow

60. shove

61. shame

62. smoke

63. raid

64. sink

65. taste

66. switch

67. shut

68. slam

69. slap

70. terrify

71. reassure

72. slice

73. sieve

74. enact

75. screen

76. film

77. devise

STEP 70
Adjectives - #2

Before we talk about adjectives, let's talk briefly about nouns. Nouns, at a basic level, are the names of places, people, or things. Here are some examples of nouns:

- dog
- John
- cord
- computer
- chair
- sky

An adjectives is a word used to modify the meaning of a noun. In other words, an adjective helps to make the meaning of a noun clearer. For example,

- A black-and-white dog
- Big John
- A long cord
- A thin computer
- A fluffy chair
- A blue-green sky

Make a sentence with each of the following words:

1. unpaid

2. sore

3. sticky

4. zealous

5. sour

6. stormy

7. dashing

8. jumpy

9. stout

10. ratty

11. acidic

12. lackadaisical

13. straight

14. decayed

15. zany

16. strange

17. large

18. adorable

19. sparkling

20. strong

21. deceitful

22. yummy

23. stunning

24. lazy

25. worried

26. substantial

27. deep

28. spicy

29. adventurous

30. successful

31. wonderful

32. lethal

33. proud

34. splendid

35. defeated

36. wobbly

37. pungent

38. agitated

39. defiant

40. puny

41. witty

42. little

43. spotless

44. quaint

45. lively

46. wicked

47. quizzical

48. alert

49. square

50. livid

51. delicious

52. lonely

53. reassured

54. delightful

STEP 71
Adjectives - #3

You probably remember that adjectives modify nouns; they give more information about nouns or pronouns. And pronouns are words that stand in for nouns.

Junko is tall; *she* is really tall.

The pronoun "she" stands in for Junko in the second part of the sentence.

Qualitative Adjectives

Adjectives may give more information about the features and qualities of things, animals, or people. For example, when you describe people or things (small, tall, long, etc.), or talk about how they are feeling (happy, sad, angry), you are talking about qualitative adjectives These can be graded, as for example,

> a very long snake
> a fairly exquisite dessert
> an unbelievably interesting movie

Adjectives may also come after the following verbs:

> taste, be, become, seem, look, smells

> The singer *seems* **cool**.
> The model *looks* **elegant**.

Classifying Adjectives

Scientists love classifying things. But it is not only scientists who classify things. We all do. You might go for a daily walk, subscribe to a biweekly newsletter, and participate in an annual parade. You may come from the northern part of your country while you take vacations in the south.

Classifying adjectives are usually not compared, as qualitative adjectives might be.

Here are some examples of classifying adjectives:

- plastic toy
- nuclear power
- quantum physics
- rough road
- analog watch
- digital camera

Adjectives that Highlight Relations Between People and Things

Janice and Amanda are **acquainted**.
The doctor was **aware** of the patient's pain.
Philadelphia is the city of **brotherly** love.

The relationship between Injira and Sanata is **broken**.
The members of the fraternity are **clannish**.
Sarah is **fond** of cats.

Hawaii is **different** from Okinawa in many ways.
Sean is **keen** on entering Harvard.
This is a **near** translation and is good enough.

June and Jane are as **thick** as thieves.
The two wrestlers are on **friendly** terms.
The two of them have a very **brittle** relationship.
This is definitely an example of a **dysfunctional** family.
His **estranged** wife tried to run him off the road.

There is a death in the family; it is not surprising then that she has such a **heavy** heart.
We have been on **speaking** terms only since last week.

Adjectives that end end in -ly

> He is quite an elderly man.
> The little girl is friendly.
> That was an unlikely encounter with a bear.

Do not use these as though they were adverbs.

Make Sentences with the Following Adjectives:

1. miserly

2. northerly

3. oily

4. orderly

5. quarterly

6. scholarly

7. sly

8. smelly

9. southerly

10. stately

11. surly

12. timely

13. unruly

14. untimely

15. unsightly

16. westerly

17. wobbly

18. woolly

19. holy

20. lively

21. lonely

22. melancholy

23. measly

24. manly

25. leisurely

26. kindly

27. jolly

28. homely

29. hilly

30. heavenly

31. grisly

32. ghostly

33. ghastly

34. easterly

35. disorderly

36. cowardly

37. chilly

38. bodily

39. unfriendly

40. deadly

41. curly

42. costly

43. ugly

44. silly

45. unlikely

46. lovely

47. likely

48. perilous

49. elderly

50. immediate

51. inseparable

52. shifting

53. intimate

54. sororal

55. interpersonal

56. strong

57. long-lost

58. suited

59. matrilineal

60. patrilineal

61. tight

62. warming

63. one-to-one

64. personal

65. unstable

66. platonic

67. related

68. rocky

69. subtle

70. asinine

Describing People

Arthur is generous.

The doctor is arrogant.

That writer is humble.

The billionaire is eccentric.

The young businesswoman is quite charismatic.

The porter was polite to us all day.

Make Sentences witht the following adjectives:

1. cruel

2. chic

3. eclectic

4. modest

5. Japanese

6. Black

7. White

8. Asian

9. Straight (hair)

10. Curly (hair)

11. Cropped (hair)

12. Creative

13. Flexible

14. Blonde

15. Tapering

16. Lanky

17. Squat

18. curvacious

19. rotund

20. clever

21. chiseled

22. plump

23. mysterious

24. cooperative

25. flamboyant

26. helpful

27. special

28. salient

29. outstanding

30. sharp-witted

31. unusual

32. diagnostic

33. useful

34. talkative

35. desirable

36. relevant

37. prominent

38. delicate

39. natural

40. notable

41. conspicuous

42. dominant

43. distinct

44. heavy

45. red

46. ugly

47. hot

48. wet

49. witty

50. sarcastic

51. salacious

Describe States

Make a sentence with each of the following words and phrases:

1. beat-up

2. damaged

3. cleansed

4. elated

5. happy

6. relaxed

7. bent

8. nervous

9. ashamed

10. angry

11. closed

12. open

13. controversial

14. confused

15. excited

16. blemished

17. energetic

18. tired

19. bored

20. occupied

21. busted

22. dinged

23. flawed

24. fouled up

25. glitchy

26. impaired

27. imperfect

28. wrong

29. organized

30. dirty

31. happy

32. cheerful

33. in need of repair

34. in poor condition

35. in smithereens

36. injured

37. kaput

38. loused up

39. marred

40. out of action

41. out of kilter

42. out of whack

43. on the blink

44. on the fritz

45. screwed up

46. shot

47. snafu

48. spoiled

49. sunk

50. totaled

51. unsound

52. fixed

53. mended

54. perfect

55. repaired

56. working

57. unbroken

58. undamaged

Describing the State of People's Hair
Make sentences to demonstrate your understanding of the following:

1. scraggly

2. nappy

3. matted

4. luxuriant

5. loose

6. lanky

7. hairy

8. hairless

9. fuzzy

10. flyaway

11. balding

12. bald

13. flowing

14. have a bad hair day (noun)

15. down to (her waist, her shoulder, etc.)

16. wiry

17. windswept

18. wind-blown

19. wavy

20. unkempt

21. disheveled

22. curl (noun)

23. curly

24. coiffured

25. coiffed

26, bushy

27. bristly

28. body (noun)

29. tousled

30. tidy

31. thin on top

32. thin

33. thick

34. swept back

35. split ends (noun)

36. spiky

37. sleek

38. shaggy

39. gaunt

STEP 72

Postpositive Adjectives

Many of the adjectives we have encountered come <u>before</u> the noun. We speak for example of a **red** light, a **wooden** table, or a **leather** belt.

Some adjectives can be placed after the noun. Here are some examples:

> The words <u>unspoken</u> hung between the two former lovers like a cloud.
> I prayed to God <u>almighty</u> to help me pass the test.
> I never worry my head over matters <u>unknown</u>.
> We have not been paying enough attention to our accounts <u>payable</u>.

There are many such phrases in English that come almost ready made (set phrases). If you are familiar with them, you can pick them out in a test.

Demonstrate your understanding of the following by making sentences.

1. things innumerable

2. something useful

2. arms akimbo

3. those responsible

4. times past

5. battle royal

6. eyes wide open

7. heir apparent

8. town proper

9. shortest route possible

10. the worst conditions imaginable

11. water aplenty

12. best room available

13. life everlasting

14. flowers galore

15. creatures unseen

16. proof positive

17. parts unknown

18. arms wide open

19. all those entering

20. the best cabin available

21. the people liable

22. the payment due

23. the city proper

24. every star visible

25. the people responsible

STEP 73

Multiple Adjectives: Order

Which of the following is correct? Young black people or black young people? A metal red thin gadget or a thin red metal gadget? A gold thick long comb or a long thick gold comb?

These can pose problems especially when native speakers, in spite of any rules you may see in a textbook, sometimes break the rules. Check this out:

a) As a civil rights lawyer, activist, legal scholar and mother of three black children, I could not wait to read what Coates had to say to **black young people** at this moment in hour history...
          Michelle Alexander (Ta-Nehisi Coates's 'Between the World and Me'New York Times, Aug 17, 2015

b) She worries about being cast as an interpreter or go-to spokeswoman for **young black people,** she said.
          Alexander Alter ('The Mothers,' a Debut Novel, Is Already Creating a Stir / New York Times, Oct. 9 2016)

As you read, pay attention to how careful communicators use words, and follow suit. In the above examples, we might say that both are correct. Sometimes, there is more than one way to express an idea. The tables and rules are just a guide. You will find that not everyone follows them all the time.

Some textbooks offer tables to help you learn the correct order of adjectives. This can be helpful, but it's probably not the most effective way to learn. Paying attention to how good writers or speakers use multiple adjectives is a much better way.

But, you need to be familiar with these tables, just in case you're the kind of person who relies on such rules.

Opinion adjectives

When you are dealing with opinion adjectives, it is suggested that you put your opinion before the adjective that describes the object.

Opinion	Descriptor	Noun
Fabulous	comfortable	sofa
Lovely	cosy	house
Naughty	little	chap
Nice	clean	skirt

Descriptive adjectives

Size	Shape	Age	Color	Nationality	Material	Noun
large	round	old	red	Turkish	leather	seat

As you realize, this is only a guide. It works most of the time, but there are times when you will see one writer put shape before physical quality or an order that does not strictly agree with the above.

If you become an avid reader, you will get a sense of what is right and what is not. That way, you can become a part of those who shape the English language rather than always waiting for someone to declare what is right or wrong. If you follow the above rules, it would mean having to say beautiful big butterfly but in reality it's much more common to say, big beautiful butterfly. Use the rules only as a rough guide; you are better off absorbing the realities of the language through extensive reading!

Exercise: Make a sentence with each of the following phrases.

1. blue tassel leather strap

2. big beautiful butterfly

3. yellow clay French soap dish

4. lucky brown dog

5. big brown race horse

6. tall amusing Hungarian teacher

7. first African-American president

8. royal wedding party

9. Malaysian anti-graft investigators

10. a 1.80 metre (5ft 11 in) Brazilian supermodel

STEP 74

Absolute Adjectives

She is good at baking bread. You are better at baking bread. I'm the best at baking bread.

The above is a typical example of the use of an adjective (good), that is gradable into the comparative (better) and the superlative (the best).

There are adjectives that cannot usually be graded in this way.

We cannot say, for example, that "Leila is a little pregnant." If she is pregnant, she is pregnant. If she is not pregnant, she is not pregnant. There is no room for a little or a lot.

Some of these absolute adjectives include perfect, unique, and idea. As such, you do not want to say, "That singer is very unique." Despite this rule, you may have heard of an American president talking about developing "a more perfect union."

A person is either alive or dead. And yet, in the New York Times, we read, "In poetry our familiar language can start to feel resonant with significance, more alive, even noble." (Matthew Zapruder, "Understanding Poetry is More Straightforward Than You Think." July 10, 2017, New York Times).

Rules alone are not enough. You should read extensively, so that you get to understand the music of the language. The rules are great, but they are not everything.

Exercise:

Make sentences to demonstrate your understanding of the following adjectives.

1. whole

2. dead

3. inevitable

4. absolute

5. impossible

6. sufficient

7. preferable

8. ideal

9. universal

10. final

11. unique

12. fatal

13. minor

14. unavoidable

15. entire

16. absent

17. accurate

18. active

19. boundless

20. settled

21. certain

22. cognizant

23. confirmed

24. communal

25. conclusive

26. fearful

27. critical

28. defeated

29. deficient

30. contiguous

31. devastated

32. devoid

33. different

34. dire

35. dispensable

36. domestic

37. drenched

38. effective

39. empty

40. enough

41. essential

42. established

43. eternal

44. everyday

45. foremost

46. foreseeable

47. frequent

48. full

49. functional

50. evident

51. greatest

52. harmless

53. hopeful

54. hopeless

STEP 75
Adverbs - #1

Adverbs give extra information about verbs, adjectives, or other adverbs. Adverbs are famous for being formed by the addition of -ly to an adjective.

Adjective	Adverb
main	mainly
fortunate	fortunately
quick	quickly
calm	calmly
beautiful	beautifully
careful	carefully
hopeful	hopefully
lucky	luckily
extreme	extremely

Adverbs that end in -ward (expressing spatial or temporal direction)

- inwards
- eastwards
- upwards
- downwards
- toward
- seaward
- afterward

Adverbs that end in -wise (expressing manner, position, direction, reference, etc.)

clockwise

counterclockwise

likewise

lengthwise

edgewise

timewise

marketwise

Adverbs that look like Adjectives: Same Form

Adjective		Adverb	
hard	(hard bargain)	hard	(hit the ball hard)
fast	(fast car)	fast	(run fast)
outside	(outside counsel)	outside	(go outside)
monthly	(monthly allowance)		
	(pay me monthly)		

Note the difference in adjective and adverb forms

back	She leaned back to ponder the question. (Adverb)
	The back door is closed. (Adjective)
only	He only looked at one sample. (adverb)
	You are the only person elected for the job. (Adjective)
very	He spoke very slowly. (Adverb)
	That's the very fabric I was looking for. (Adjective)

Make Two Sentences, One with the Adjective and the Other, with the Adverb.

1.

WORDS	Sentences
Adjective abnormal	
Adverb abnormally	

2.

WORDS	Sentences
Adjective wide	
Adverb widely	

3.

WORDS	Sentences
Adjective low	
Adverb lowly	

4.

WORDS	Sentences
Adjective diligent	
Adverb diligently	

5.

WORDS	Sentences
Adjective right	
Adverb rightly	

6.

WORDS	Sentences
Adjective hopeless	
Adverb hopelessly	

7.

WORDS	Sentences
Adjective near	
Adverb nearly	

8.

WORDS	Sentences
Adjective rightful	
Adverb rightfully	

9.

WORDS	Sentences
Adjective ultimate	
Adverb ultimately	

10.

WORDS	Sentences
Adjective rigid	
Adverb rigidly	

11.

WORDS	Sentences
Adjective neat	
Adverb neatly	

12.

WORDS	Sentences
Adjective free	
Adverb freely	

13.

WORDS	Sentences
Adjective dim	
Adverb dimly	

14

WORDS	Sentences
Adjective accident	
Adverb accidentally	

15.

WORDS	Sentences
Adjective doubtful	
Adverb doubtfully	

16.

WORDS	Sentences
Adjective truthful	
Adverb truthfully	

Make sentences with the following adverbs.

1. righteously

2. naturally

3. honestly

4. delightfully

5. deliberately

6. highly

7. mostly

8. mysteriously

9. reproachfully

10. triumphantly

11. zestfully

12. zealously

13. defiantly

14. helplessly

15. mortally

16. repeatedly

17. tremendously

18. youthfully

19. deeply

20. dearly

21. deceptively

22. daintily

23. curiously

24. cruelly

25. crossly

26. courageously

27. correctly

28. coolly

29. continually

30. commonly

31. actually

32. adventurously

33. afterwards

34. almost

35. always

36. annually

37. anxiously

38. arrogantly

39. awkwardly

40. bashfully

41. beautifully

42. bitterly

43. bleakly

44. blindly

45. boastfully

46. boldly

47. briefly

48. bravely

49. brightly

50. briskly

51. broadly

52. busily

53. calmly

54. carefully

55. carelessly

56. cautiously

57. certainly

58. cheerfully

59. clearly

60. closely

61. coaxingly

62. colorfully

63. unaccountably

64. upward

65. urgently

66. usefully

67. uselessly

68. usually

69. utterly

70. vacantly

71. vaguely

72. vainly

73. valiantly

74. vastly

75. verbally

76. fashionably

77. viciously

78. victoriously

79. violently

80. vivaciously

81. vicariously

82. voluntarily

83. warmly

84. weakly

85. wearily

86. well

87. wetly

88. wholly

89. wildly

90. willfully

91. wisely

92. woefully

93. wonderfully

94. worriedly

95. wrongly

96. yawningly

97. yearly

98. yearningly

99. yesterday

100. youthfully

101. immediately

102. innocently

103. inquisitively

104. instantly

105. intensely

106. intently

107. interestingly

108. inwardly

109. irritably

110. jaggedly

111. jealously

112. jovially

113. joyfully

114. jubilantly

115. judgmentally

116. justly

117. keenly

118. kiddingly

119. kindheartedly

120. kindly

121. readily

122. naturally

123. knowingly

124. knowledgeably

125. kookily

126. lazily

127. less

128. lightly

129. likely

130. limply

131. loftily

STEP 76

Let's Get Physical

1.

Word	Meaning
somatic	
	My sentence

2.

Idiom	Meaning
anatomy	
	My sentence

3.

Word	Meaning
figure	
	My sentence

4.

Word	Meaning
bodily	
	My sentence

5.

Word/Phrase	Meaning
body image	
	My sentence

6.

Word	Meaning
human	
	My sentence

7.

Word/Phrase	Meaning
biological clock	
	My sentence

8.

Word/Phrase	Meaning
from head to toe	
	My sentence

9.

Word	Meaning
internal	
	My sentence

10.

Word	Meaning
hyperactive	
	My sentence

11.

Word	Meaning
cervical	
	My sentence

12.

Word	Meaning
pectoral	
	My sentence

13.

Word	Meaning
posterior	
	My sentence

14.

Word	Meaning
topical	
	My sentence

15.

Word	Meaning
an hourglass figure	
	My sentence

16.

Word	Meaning
beefy	
	My sentence

17.

Word	Meaning
brawny	
	My sentence

18.

Word	Meaning
burly	
	My sentence

19.

Word	Meaning
gangly	
	My sentence

20.

Word	Meaning
heavy-set	
	My sentence

21.

Word	Meaning
lanky	
	My sentence

22.

Word	Meaning
muscular	
	My sentence

23.

Word	Meaning
pear-shaped	
	My sentence

24.

Word	Meaning
bionic	
	My sentence

25.

Word	Meaning
slightly-built	
	My sentence

26.

Word	Meaning
statuesque	
	My sentence

27.

Word	Meaning
strapping	
	My sentence

28.

Word	Meaning
willowy	
	My sentence

29.

Word	Meaning
thickset	
	My sentence

30.

Word	Meaning
taut	
	My sentence

31.

Word	Meaning
stooped	
	My sentence

32.

Word	Meaning
	My sentence

33.

Word	Meaning
	My sentence

34.

Word	Meaning
	My sentence

STEP 77
Adverbs - #2

1. madly

2. majestically

3. meaningfully

4. mechanically

5. merrily

6. miserably

7. mockingly

8. monthly

9. more

10. separately

11. selfishly

12. tightly

13. thoughtfully

14. thoroughly

15. thankfully

16. terribly

17. tensely

18. tenderly

19. sympathetically

20. swiftly

21. sweetly

22. suspiciously

23. surprisingly

24. suddenly

25. successfully

26. strictly

27. sternly

28. stealthily

29. speedily

30. seriously

31. sometimes

32. solidly

33. solemnly

34. slowly

35. sleepily

36. silently

37. shyly

38. sheepishly

39. sharply

40. shakily

41. seldom

42. surreptitiously

STEP 78

Adjectives - #4

Make a sentence with each of the following adjectives.

1. relieved

2. ludicrous

3. repulsive

4. depressed

5. stale

6. macho

7. responsive

8. magnificent

9. maniacal

10. eclectic

11. miniature

12. mistaken

13. annoyed

14. dizzy

15. drab

16. unsightly

17. mysterious

18. elated

19. emaciated

20. thick

21. nonchalant

22. nonsensical

23. tense

24. rough

25. aloof

26. degenerative

27. round

28. whopping

29. melancholy

30. rough

31. whimsical

32. diminutive

33. salty

34. tender

35. envious

36. nutritious

37. teeny

38. exasperated

39. average

40. tasty

41. nutty

42. craven

43. sullen

44. obedient

45. oblivious

46. exhilarated

47. timely

48. cumbersome

49. obnoxious

50. extensive

51. curved

52. odd

53. unsuccessful

54. utter

55. vulnerable

56. weighted

57. weightless

58. willful

59. worst

60. wrecked

61. wrong

62. waterlogged

63. unsightly

64. unrequited

65. unquestionable

66. unprecedented

67. unnecessary

68. unmarried

69. unlimited

70. unknown

71. uninformed

72. unimportant

73. uniform

74. unequivocal

75. unequal

76. undecided

77. unconditional

78. unclouded

79. unclear

80. unbroken

81. unbounded

82. unblemished

83. visionary

84. unanimous

85. ultimate

86. true

87. total

88. topmost

89. thorough

90. tertiary

91. temporary

92. sure

93. supreme

94. superlative

95. superfluous

96. suitable

97. straightforward

98. staunch

99. stationary

100. starving

101. square

102. spotless

103. soaked

104. smashed

105. singular

106. pompous

107. grieving

108. cheeky

109. gritty

110. pleasant

111. healthy

112. happy

113. quixotic

114. harebrained

115. handsome

116. chubby

117. melancholy

118. gigantic

119. clueless

120. gorgeous

121. glamorous

122. permitted

123. tight

124. hungry

125. hurt

126. clean

127. astonishing

128. thoughtless

129. distraught

130. hollow

131. arrogant

132. nonsensical

133. elegant

134. round

135. massive

136. huge

137. horrific

33. nutritious

138. old-fashioned

139. tense

140. homely

141. virtuous

142. aloof

143. terrible

144. rough

145. vexed

146. unparalleled

147. mortified

148. dangerous

149. uptight

150. moody

STEP 79

Let's Get Medical

1.

Word	Meaning
cure	
	My sentence

2.

Idiom	Meaning
cure-all	
	My sentence

3.

Word	Meaning
dementia	
	My sentence

4.

Word	Meaning
medication	
	My sentence

5.

Word	Meaning
i	
	My sentence

6.

Word	Meaning
panacea	
	My sentence

7.

Word	Meaning
pharmaceuticals	
	My sentence

8.

Word	Meaning
placebo	
	My sentence

9.

Word	Meaning
prescription	
	My sentence

10.

Word	Meaning
remedy	
	My sentence

11.

Word	Meaning
antenatal	
	My sentence

12.

Word	Meaning
antibacterial	
	My sentence

13.

Word	Meaning
aseptic	
	My sentence

14.

Word	Meaning
bloodless	
	My sentence

15.

Word	Meaning
clinical	
	My sentence

16.

Word/Phrase	Meaning
conventional treatment	
	My sentence

17.

Word	Meaning
diagnostic	
	My sentence

18.

Word/Phrase	Meaning
elective surgery	
	My sentence

19.

Word	Meaning
emollient	
	My sentence

20.

Word	Meaning
fast-acting	
	My sentence

21.

Word	Meaning
for external use	
	My sentence

22.

Word	Meaning
gynecological	
	My sentence

23.

Word	Meaning
habit-forming	
	My sentence

24.

Word	Meaning
hallucination	
	My sentence

25.

Word	Meaning
holistic	
	My sentence

26.

Word	Meaning
hypodermic syringe	
	My sentence

27.

Word	Meaning
intravenous	
	My sentence

28.

Word	Meaning
invasive	
	My sentence

29.

Word	Meaning
lifesaving	
	My sentence

30.

Word/Phrase	Meaning
medicated soap	
	My sentence

31.

Word	Meaning
narcotic	
	My sentence

32.

Word	Meaning
non-invasive	
	My sentence

33.

Word	Meaning
non-prescription	
	My sentence

34.

Word/Phrase	Meaning
oral medicine	
	My sentence

35.

Word	Meaning
orthopedic	
	My sentence

36.

Word/Phrase	Meaning
over the counter	
	My sentence

37.

Word	Meaning
paediatric	
	My sentence

38.

Word/Phrase	Meaning
palliative	
	My sentence

39.

Word	Meaning
postoperative	
	My sentence

40.

Word	Meaning
potent	
	My sentence

41.

Word	Meaning
prophylactic	
	My sentence

42.

Word	Meaning
prosthetic	
	My sentence

43.

Word	Meaning
psychiatric	
	My sentence

44.

Word	Meaning
sanitary	
	My sentence

45.

Word	Meaning
therapeutic	
	My sentence

46.

Word/Phrase	Meaning
go under the knife	
	My sentence

47.

Word	Meaning
accupressure	
	My sentence

48.

Word	Meaning
acupuncture	
	My sentence

49.

Word/Phrase	Meaning
alternative medicine	
	My sentence

50.

Word	Meaning
anaesthesia	
	My sentence

51.

Word	Meaning
aromatherapy	
	My sentence

52.

Word	Meaning
artificial insemination	
	My sentence

53.

Word	Meaning
aspiration	
	My sentence

54.

Word	Meaning
blood transfusion	
	My sentence

55.

Word	Meaning
chemotherapy	
	My sentence

56.

Word	Meaning
chiropractic	
	My sentence

57.

Word	Meaning
CPR cardiopulmonary resuscitation	
	My sentence

58.

Word	Meaning
detox	
	My sentence

59.

Word	Meaning
dialysis	
	My sentence

60.

Word	Meaning
enema	
	My sentence

61.

Word	Meaning
first aid	
	My sentence

62.

Word	Meaning
herbal medicine	
	My sentence

63.

Word	Meaning
homeopathy	
	My sentence

64.

Word	Meaning
HRT hormone replacement therapy	
	My sentence

65.

Word	Meaning
hypnotherapy	
	My sentence

66.

Word	Meaning
incision	
	My sentence

67.

Word	Meaning
internal medicine	
	My sentence

68.

Word/Phrase	Meaning
the kiss of life	
	My sentence

69.

Word	Meaning
life support	
	My sentence

70.

Word	Meaning
occupational therapy	
	My sentence

71.

Word	Meaning
primary care	
	My sentence

72.

Word	Meaning
quackery	
	My sentence

73.

Word	Meaning
radiology	
	My sentence

74.

Word	Meaning
regimen	
	My sentence

STEP 80

Idiomatic Expressions - #4

1.

Idiom	listen to reason
Meaning	
Sample sentence/ My sentence	

2.

Idiom	cut against the grain
Meaning	
Sample sentence/ My sentence	

3.

Idiom	in the dark about something
Meaning	
Sample sentence/ My sentence	

4.

Idiom	abandon ship
Meaning	
Sample sentence/ My sentence	

5.

Idiom	in the ballpark
Meaning	
Sample sentence/ My sentence	

6.

Idiom	above the fray
Meaning	
Sample sentence/ My sentence	

7.

Idiom	in good company
Meaning	
Sample sentence/ My sentence	

8.

Idiom	Achilles' heel
Meaning	
Sample sentence/ My sentence	

9.

Idiom	hedge one's bets
Meaning	
Sample sentence/ My sentence	

10.

Idiom	afraid of one's own shadow
Meaning	
Sample sentence/ My sentence	

11.

Idiom	have one's finger in too many pies
Meaning	
Sample sentence/ My sentence	

12.

Idiom	have a close call
Meaning	
Sample sentence/ My sentence	

13.

Idiom	hail a cab
Meaning	
Sample sentence/ My sentence	

14.

Idiom	all ears
Meaning	
Sample sentence/ My sentence	

15.

Idiom	gut feeling
Meaning	
Sample sentence/ My sentence	

16.

Idiom	go under the knife
Meaning	
Sample sentence/ My sentence	

17.

Idiom	a glutton for punishment
Meaning	
Sample sentence/ My sentence	

18.

Idiom	all walks of life
Meaning	
Sample sentence/ My sentence	

19.

Idiom	answer to someone
Meaning	
Sample sentence/ My sentence	

20.

Idiom	asleep at the wheel
Meaning	
Sample sentence/ My sentence	

21.

Idiom	at the top of one's game
Meaning	
Sample sentence/ My sentence	

22.

Idiom	back to square one
Meaning	
Sample sentence/ My sentence	

23.

Idiom	a basket case
Meaning	
Sample sentence/ My sentence	

24.

Idiom	get down to business
Meaning	
Sample sentence/ My sentence	

STEP 81

Adjectives - #5

1. vast

2. disturbed

3. distressed

4. fancy

5. secondary

6. saturated

7. ruthless

8. ruined

9. rudimentary

10. round

11. right

12. revocable

13. requited

14. replete

15. redundant

16. rare

17. pure

18. public

19. proximate

20. private

21. principal

22. primitive

23. primary

24. preventable

25. present

26. premeditated

27. preeminent

28. sheer

29. shattered

30. set

31. sentient

32. secondary

33. satisfactory

34. predominant

35. precise

36. powerless

37. possible

38. popular

39. pivotal

40. perpetual

41. passable

42. partial

43. paramount

44. packed

45. overwhelmed

46. overstocked

47. overjoyed

48. overheated

49. overflowing

50. overall

51. outright

52. outermost

53. opposite

54. operational

55. opaque

56. omnipresent

57. omnipotent

58. energetic

59. enormous

60. batty

61. antsy

62. motionless

63. muddy

64. anxious

65. enchanting

66. thankful

67. encouraging

68. nervous

69. testy

70. fantastic

71. sweet

72. fierce

73. swanky

74. outrageous

75. beefy

76. scant

77. superior

78. cruel

79. filthy

80. scary

81. superficial

82. crooked

83. scattered

84. bewildered

85. succulent

86. creepy

87. responsive

88. weary

89. amiable

90. sarcastic

91. melted

92. apprehensive

93. embarrassed

94. thoughtful

95. ashamed

96. vivacious

97. steady

98. determined

99. ripe

100. wacky

111. robust

112. rotten

113. steep

114. vivacious

115. dilapidated

116. rotund

117. perceptive

118. enthusiastic

119. uneven

120. drained

121. narrow

122. troubled

123. nasty

124. dull

125. trite

126. appalling

127. eager

128. obvious

129. obscure

130. needless

131. multiple

132. mortal

133. minimal

134. midway

135. middle

136. merciless

137. melting

138. meaningless

139. meaningful

140. maximal

141. matchless

142. matching

143. married

144. manifest

145. malfunctioning

146. lowermost

147. local

148. literally

149. lighted

150. joint

STEP 82

Let's Get Legal

1.

Word	Meaning
criminal	
	My sentence

2.

Idiom	Meaning
forensic	
	My sentence

3.

Word	Meaning
judicial	
	My sentence

4.

Word	Meaning
juvenile	
	My sentence

5.

Word	Meaning
legislative	
	My sentence

6.

Word	Meaning
liable	
	My sentence

7.

Word	Meaning
retroactive	
	My sentence

8.

Word	Meaning
statutory	
	My sentence

9.

Word	Meaning
valid	
	My sentence

10.

Word	Meaning
unproven	
	My sentence

11.

Word	Meaning
void	
	My sentence

12.

Word	Meaning
arson	
	My sentence

13.

Word	Meaning
caveat emptor	
	My sentence

14.

Word	Meaning
contraband	
	My sentence

15.

Word	Meaning
extradition	
	My sentence

16.

Word	Meaning
incarcerate	
	My sentence

17.

Word	Meaning
perpetrator	
	My sentence

18.

Word	Meaning
litigation	
	My sentence

19.

Word	Meaning
plaintiff	
	My sentence

20.

Word	Meaning
probation	
	My sentence

21.

Word	Meaning
prosecutor	
	My sentence

22.

Word	Meaning
injunction	
	My sentence

23.

Word	Meaning
subpoena	
	My sentence

24.

Word	Meaning
larceny	
	My sentence

STEP 83

Adverbs - #3

Please use each of the following words to make a sentence.

1. seemingly

2. sedately

3. searchingly

4. scarily

5. scarcely

6. safely

7. rudely

8. roughly

9. faithfully

10. energetically

11. enormously

12. emphatically

13. equally

14. evenly

15. eventually

16. exactly

17. excitedly

18. extremely

19. fairly

20. faithfully

21. far

22. fast

23. ferociously

24. fatally

25. freely

26. frenetically

27. frightfully

28. fully

29. furiously

30. generally

31. gently

32. gladly

33. gleefully

34. gracefully

35. gratefully

36. greatly

37. greedily

38. happily

39. hastily

40. healthily

41. heavily

42. helpfully

43. nervously

44. nicely

45. noisily

46. obediently

47. obnoxiously

48. oddly

49. offensively

50. officially

51. only

52. openly

53. reluctantly

54. regularly

55. recklessly

56. reassuringly

57. really

58. rarely

59. rapidly

60. randomly

61. quizzically

62. quirkily

63. quietly

64. quickly

65. questionably

66. queerly

67. queasily

68. quaintly

69. punctually

70. properly

71. promptly

72. powerfully

73. potentially

74. positively

75. poorly

76. politely

77. playfully

78. physically

79. perfectly

80. patiently

81. partially

82. painfully

83. overconfidently

84. optimistically

85. openly

STEP 84

Let's Get Scientific

1.

Word	Meaning
aerodynamic	
	My sentence

2.

Word	Meaning
astronomy	
	My sentence

3.

Word	Meaning
bacteriology	
	My sentence

4.

Word	Meaning
buoyancy	
	My sentence

5.

Word	Meaning
dermatology	
	My sentence

6.

Word	Meaning
ecology	
	My sentence

7.

Word	Meaning
electronics	
	My sentence

8.

Word	Meaning
meteorology	
	My sentence

9.

Word	Meaning
metallurgy	
	My sentence

10.

Word	Meaning
mycology	
	My sentence

11.

Word	Meaning
oceanography	
	My sentence

12.

Word	Meaning
philology	
	My sentence

13.

Word	Meaning
optics	
	My sentence

14.

Word	Meaning
seismology	
	My sentence

15.

Word	Meaning
STEM science, technology, engineering, math	
	My sentence

16.

Word	Meaning
toxicology	
	My sentence

17.

Word	Meaning
zoology	
	My sentence

18.

Word	Meaning
biodiversity	
	My sentence

19.

Word	Meaning
pathogen	
	My sentence

20.

Word	Meaning
physiological	
	My sentence

21.

Word/Phrase	Meaning
chain reaction	
	My sentence

22.

Word	Meaning
elasticity	
	My sentence

23.

Word	Meaning
equilibrium	
	My sentence

24.

Word	Meaning
metal fatigue	
	My sentence

25.

Word	Meaning
friction	
	My sentence

26.

Word	Meaning
fusion	
	My sentence

27.

Word	Meaning
gravity	
	My sentence

28.

Word	Meaning
inertia	
	My sentence

29.

Word	Meaning
insulation	
	My sentence

30.

Word	Meaning
locomotive	
	My sentence

31.

Word	Meaning
momentum	
	My sentence

32.

Word	Meaning
propulsion	
	My sentence

33.

Word	Meaning
suction	
	My sentence

34.

Word	Meaning
thrust	
	My sentence

35.

Word	Meaning
traction	
	My sentence

36.

Word	Meaning
heritable	
	My sentence

37.

Word	Meaning
gene	
	My sentence

38.

Word	Meaning
inbreeding	
	My sentence

39.

Word	Meaning
infanticide	
	My sentence

STEP 85

Adjectives - #5

Please use each of the following words to make a sentence.

1. irrevocable

2. inactive

3. inaccurate

4. immediate

5. incomplete

6. incorrect

7. incorrigible

8. ineffable

9. inconsistent

10. invulnerable

11. invalid

12. insufficient

13. insincere

14. innocent

15. ingrained

16. informed

17. infinite

18. inferior

19. inexact

20. inevitable

21. inert

22. individual

23. indispensable

24. incurable

25. incomparable

26. tricky

27. naughty

28. ecstatic

29. appetizing

30. scrawny

31. biting

32. successful

33. flat

34. substantial

35. crabby

36. unrealistic

37. floppy

38. shaggy

39. bitter

40. strong

41. courageous

42. bland

43. shaky

44. shallow

45. sharp

46. shiny

47. short

48. silky

49. silly

50. smarmy

51. smiling

52. strange

53. straight

54. costly

55. stout

56. foolish

57. independent

58. stormy

59. skinny

60. slimy

61. slippery

62. smoggy

63. corny

64. bored

65. sticky

66. frantic

67. brave

68. depraved

69. disgusted

70. vivid

71. mammoth

72. distinct

73. minute

74. cooperative

75. abrupt

76. cumbersome

77. bright

78. cruel

79. fresh

80. convoluted

81. crooked

82. friendly

83. broad

84. convincing

85. frightened

86. contemplative

87. cynical

88. frothy

89. smooth

90. smug

91. panicky

92. perfect

93. confused

94. dangerous

95. frustrating

96. condescending

97. dashing

98. funny

99. decayed

100. condemned

101. gaudy

102. soggy

103. solid

104. deceitful

105. comfortable

106. deep

107. defeated

108. defiant

109. combative

110. joyous

111. gentle

112. jolly

113. colossal

114. jittery

115. ghastly

116. jealous

117. colorful

118. giddy

119. greasy

120. grieving

121. cloudy

122. itchy

123. irritable

124. irate

125. intrigued

126. clear

127. impressionable

128. immense

129. intriguing

130. icy

131. cheerful

132. high

133. helpless

134. progressive

135. helpful

136. grumpy

137. charming

138. petite

139. petty

140. plain

141. burly

142. grubby

143. poised

144. grotesque

145. bulky

146. victorious

147. misty

148. differential

149. intrinsic

150. comparative

151. adaptive

STEP 86
Words Relating to Women

1.

Word	Meaning
female	
	My sentence

2.

Word	Meaning
feminine	
	My sentence

3.

Word	Meaning
womanhood	
	My sentence

4.

Word	Meaning
matriarchal	
	My sentence

5.

Word	Meaning
matronly	
	My sentence

6.

Word	Meaning
queenly	
	My sentence

7.

Word	Meaning
mansplaining	
	My sentence

8.

Word	Meaning
feminist	
	My sentence

9.

Word	Meaning
maternity	
	My sentence

10.

Word	Meaning
marital	
	My sentence

11.

Idiom	Meaning
suffrage	
	My sentence

12.

Word	Meaning
misogynist	
	My sentence

13.

Word/Phrase	Meaning
a damsel in distress	
	My sentence

14.

Word	Meaning
homemaker	
	My sentence

15.

Word	Meaning
belle of the ball	
	My sentence

16.

Word	Meaning
widow	
	My sentence

17.

Word	Meaning
dowager	
	My sentence

18.

Word	Meaning
fertile	
	My sentence

19.

Word	Meaning
barren	
	My sentence

20.

Word	Meaning
bride	
	My sentence

21.

Word	Meaning
frumpy	
	My sentence

22.

Word	Meaning
sassy	
	My sentence

23.

Word	Meaning
voluptuous	
	My sentence

24.

Word	Meaning
lithe	
	My sentence

STEP 87

Words Relating to Men

1.

Word	Meaning
pocket square	
	My sentence

2.

Word	Meaning
male-dominated	
	My sentence

3.

Word	Meaning
masculine	
	My sentence

4.

Word	Meaning
effeminate	
	My sentence

5.

Word	Meaning
macho	
	My sentence

6.

Word	Meaning
effete	
	My sentence

7.

Word	Meaning
emasculate	
	My sentence

8.

Word	Meaning
manhood	
	My sentence

9.

Word	Meaning
gentleman	
	My sentence

10.

Word	Meaning
fellow	
	My sentence

11.

Word/Phrase	Meaning
family man	
	My sentence

12.

Word/Phrase	Meaning
a father figure	
	My sentence

13.

Word/Phrase	Meaning
a man's man	
	My sentence

14.

Word/Phrase	Meaning
double-breasted blazer	
	My sentence

15.

Word	Meaning
eunuch	
	My sentence

16.

Word	Meaning
gallant	
	My sentence

17.

Word	Meaning
lad	
	My sentence

18.

Word	Meaning
hombre	
	My sentence

19.

Word/Phrase	Meaning
mommy's boy	
	My sentence

20.

Word	Meaning
punk	
	My sentence

21.

Word	Meaning
renaissance man	
	My sentence

22.

Word	Meaning
boy wonder	
	My sentence

23.

Word	Meaning
widower	
	My sentence

24.

Word/Phrase	Meaning
man up	
	My sentence

25.

Word	Meaning
rugged	
	My sentence

26.

Word	Meaning
patriarchy	
	My sentence

27.

Word	Meaning
paternal leave	
	My sentence

28.

Word	Meaning
patrimony	
	My sentence

29.

Word	Meaning
man cave	
	My sentence

STEP 88

Let's Get Athletic

1.

Word	Meaning
battle of nerves	
	My sentence

2.

Idiom	Meaning
championship	
	My sentence

3.

Word	Meaning
clash	
	My sentence

4.

Word	Meaning
close season	
	My sentence

5.

Word	Meaning
contest	
	My sentence

6.

Word	Meaning
curtain raiser	
	My sentence

7.

Word	Meaning
derby	
	My sentence

8.

Word	Meaning
enclosure	
	My sentence

9.

Word	Meaning
draw	
	My sentence

10.

Word/Phrase	Meaning
feeding frenzy	
	My sentence

11.

Word	Meaning
grand slam	
	My sentence

12.

Word	Meaning
grudge match	
	My sentence

13.

Word	Meaning
heat	
	My sentence

14.

Word	Meaning
mismatch	
	My sentence

15.

Word	Meaning
pentathlon	
	My sentence

16.

Word	Meaning
play-off	
	My sentence

17.

Word	Meaning
pro-am	
	My sentence

18.

Word	Meaning
quarter-final	
	My sentence

19.

Word	Meaning
rematch	
	My sentence

20.

Word	Meaning
rodeo	
	My sentence

21.

Word/Phrase	Meaning
round robin	
	My sentence

22.

Word	Meaning
pole position	
	My sentence

23.

Word	Meaning
semifinal	
	My sentence

24.

Word	Meaning
series	
	My sentence

25.

Word	Meaning
showdown	
	My sentence

26.

Word	Meaning
tournament	
	My sentence

27.

Word	Meaning
trial	
	My sentence

28.

Word	Meaning
weightlifting	
	My sentence

29.

Word	Meaning
triathlon	
	My sentence

30.

Word	Meaning
track and field	
	My sentence

31.

Word	Meaning
the pole vault	
	My sentence

32.

Word	Meaning
hurdles	
	My sentence

33.

Word	Meaning
discus	
	My sentence

34.

Word	Meaning
decathlon	
	My sentence

35.

Word	Meaning
cross-country	
	My sentence

36.

Word/Phrase	Meaning
spectator sport	
	My sentence

37.

Word/Phrase	Meaning
extreme sport	
	My sentence

38.

Word	Meaning
an away game	
	My sentence

39.

Word/Phrase	Meaning
a friendly game	
	My sentence

STEP 89

Words Relating to Travel

1.

Word	Meaning
backpacking	
	My sentence

2.

Idiom	Meaning
independent travel	
	My sentence

3.

Word	Meaning
sightseeing	
	My sentence

4.

Word	Meaning
bird of passage	
	My sentence

5.

Word	Meaning
business traveler	
	My sentence

6.

Word	Meaning
commuter	
	My sentence

7.

Word	Meaning
explorer	
	My sentence

8.

Word/Phrase	Meaning
fellow traveler	
	My sentence

9.

Word	Meaning
frequent flyer	
	My sentence

10.

Word	Meaning
itinerary	
	My sentence

11.

Word	Meaning
leisure traveler	
	My sentence

12.

Word	Meaning
passenger manifest	
	My sentence

13.

Word	Meaning
pathfinder	
	My sentence

14.

Word	Meaning
pilgrim	
	My sentence

15.

Word	Meaning
roadie	
	My sentence

16.

Word	Meaning
sales representative	
	My sentence

17.

Word	Meaning
sightseer	
	My sentence

18.

Word	Meaning
vacationer	
	My sentence

19.

Word	Meaning
holidaymaker	
	My sentence

20.

Word	Meaning
vagabond	
	My sentence

21.

Word	Meaning
voyager	
	My sentence

22.

Word	Meaning
wayfarer	
	My sentence

23.

Word	Meaning
hitch	
	My sentence

24.

Word	Meaning
travel journal	
	My sentence

25.

Word	Meaning
traipse	
	My sentence

26.

Word/Phrase	Meaning
thumb a lift/ride	
	My sentence

27.

Word	Meaning
cruise	
	My sentence

28.

Word	Meaning
en route	
	My sentence

29.

Word	Meaning
negotiate a road	
	My sentence

30.

Word	Meaning
along the way	
	My sentence

31.

Word	Meaning
on the move	
	My sentence

32.

Word	Meaning
ride shotgun	
	My sentence

33.

Word/Phrase	Meaning
steer a course	
	My sentence

34.

Word/Phrase	Meaning
bus around	
	My sentence

35.

Word	Meaning
bike around	
	My sentence

36.

Word	Meaning
air traffic control	
	My sentence

37.

Word	Meaning
baggage handler	
	My sentence

38.

Word	Meaning
cabin crew	
	My sentence

39.

Word	Meaning
public transport	
	My sentence

40.

Word	Meaning
wanderlust	
	My sentence

41.

Word	Meaning
flight attendant	
	My sentence

42.

Word	Meaning
ground crew	
	My sentence

43.

Word	Meaning
skycap	
	My sentence

44.

Word	Meaning
sky marshal	
	My sentence

45.

Word	Meaning
port of call	
	My sentence

46.

Word	Meaning
well traveled	
	My sentence

47.

Word	Meaning
the jet set	
	My sentence

48.

Word	Meaning
skeleton service	
	My sentence

49.

Word	Meaning
destination	
	My sentence

50.

Word	Meaning
full board	
	My sentence

51.

Word	Meaning
splash out	
	My sentence

52.

Word	Meaning
accommodation	
	My sentence

53.

Word	Meaning
hammock	
	My sentence

54.

Word	Meaning
base jumping	
	My sentence

STEP 90

Let's Get Academic

1.

Word	Meaning
applied	
	My sentence

2.

Word/Phrase	Meaning
be an education for someone	
	My sentence

3.

Word	Meaning
banding	
	My sentence

4.

Word	Meaning
educational	
	My sentence

5.

Word	Meaning
formal	
	My sentence

6.

Word	Meaning
hands-on	
	My sentence

7.

Word	Meaning
in-service training	
	My sentence

8.

Word	Meaning
inter-disciplinary	
	My sentence

9.

Word	Meaning
multi-disciplinary	
	My sentence

10.

Word	Meaning
pedagogical	
	My sentence

11.

Word	Meaning
postgraduate	
	My sentence

12.

Word	Meaning
professorial	
	My sentence

13.

Word	Meaning
remedial	
	My sentence

14.

Word	Meaning
self-educated	
	My sentence

15.

Word	Meaning
specialist	
	My sentence

16.

Word	Meaning
under someone's tutelage	
	My sentence

17.

Word	Meaning
acquisition	
	My sentence

18.

Word	Meaning
vocational	
	My sentence

19.

Word	Meaning
well-rounded	
	My sentence

20.

Word	Meaning
autodidact	
	My sentence

21.

Word	Meaning
assimilation	
	My sentence

22.

Word	Meaning
cognitive style	
	My sentence

23.

Word	Meaning
insight	
	My sentence

24.

Word	Meaning
intensive	
	My sentence

25.

Word	Meaning
learning curve	
	My sentence

26.

Word	Meaning
lifelong learning	
	My sentence

27.

Word	Meaning
self-taught	
	My sentence

28.

Word	Meaning
teachable moment	
	My sentence

29.

Word	Meaning
trial and error	
	My sentence

30.

Word	Meaning
master something	
	My sentence

31.

Word	Meaning
absorb	
	My sentence

32.

Word	Meaning
pick up	
	My sentence

33.

Word	Meaning
retrain	
	My sentence

34.

Word	Meaning
acquaint yourself with something	
	My sentence

35.

Word	Meaning
acquire	
	My sentence

36.

Word	Meaning
get the hang of something	
	My sentence

37.

Word	Meaning
get a feeling for something	
	My sentence

38.

Word	Meaning
improve oneself	
	My sentence

39.

Word	Meaning
keep up	
	My sentence

40.

Word	Meaning	
learn the hard way		
	My sentence	

41.

Word	Meaning	
orient yourself		
	My sentence	

42.

Word	Meaning	
piece together		
	My sentence	

43.

Word	Meaning	
polish one's skills		
	My sentence	

44.

Word	Meaning	
sit at someone's feet		
	My sentence	

45.

Word	Meaning	
take to something like a duck to water		
	My sentence	

46.

Word	Meaning	
unlearn		
	My sentence	

47.

Word	Meaning	
wise up		
	My sentence	

48.

Word	Meaning	
op-ed (page opposite the editorial page)		
	My sentence	

49.

Word	Meaning	
iteration		
	My sentence	

STEP 91

Phrases Galore - Sentence Writing Practice - #1

Form sentences with each of the following to demonstrate your understanding.

1	ready for	35	listen to
2	sign up for	36	perform well on
3	identical to	37	guided through
4	on the desk	38	depend on
5	want to	39	wish to
6	on the screen	40	during the test
7	take a break	41	when you resume
8	on the test	42	on a break
9	move forward to	43	click on
10	evaluate the performance	44	prepare for
11	go awry	45	succeed in
12	around the world	46	communicate in
13	communicate effectively	47	the most accessible
14	likely that	48	cast a pall over
15	check with	49	is impassable
16	fond memories	50	apply as
17	vary from	51	in each section
18	putting away	52	perform on the test
19	tips on how to improve	53	in the book
20	designed to assess	54	sweeping with a broom
21	successful in	55	engage someone in
22	looks delicious	56	occur in
23	listen to	57	take place
24	get an aisle seat	58	get a window seat
25	listen for	59	provides service to
26	plan how to	60	cross the field
27	near the street	61	through practice
28	on the mountain	62	concentrate on
29	open to the public from	63	learn to
30	work on	64	fully opened
31	think about	65	attempt to
32	focus on	66	plan to play
33	look under the hood	67	low-hanging fruit
34	lose one's train of thought	68	make a beeline for someone/something

69	drive past		111	look delicious
70	the best way to		112	engage someone in
71	how to connect		113	take place
72	in response to		114	listen to
73	able to		115	provide service to
74	the full range of		116	communicate with
75	cover the area		117	draw upon
76	time limit for		118	cross the field
77	expected to		119	plan how to
78	allow you to		120	signs are posted
79	not need		121	help someone do
80	allotted for		122	enrol in
81	ability to		123	work on
82	arrive on time		124	be my guest
83	related to		125	learn to
84	get a window seat		126	open to
85	fully opened		127	concentrate on
86	a variety of		128	on the mountain
87	classified into		129	unbelievably difficult
88	can be obtained by		130	until it's completed
89	not too terrible		131	not so expensive
90	offer great savings		132	extremely expensive
91	very meticulous		133	way too high
92	upset about		134	a great new look
93	incredibly mesmerizing		135	coming out in torrents
94	pass (something) along		136	quite tempting
95	extremely tired		137	point out
96	fairly bored		138	weather report
97	covered in dirt		139	exposed to
98	far too serious		140	meddle with
99	beautifully stitched		141	very low
100	quite enamoured with		142	given that
101	merely anxious		143	great value
102	essential part		144	angry about
103	could mean		145	awfully bad
104	fully cooperate		146	another chance to
105	extraordinary-looking		147	raise questions
106	all ability levels		148	on behalf of
107	not necessarily		149	the fact that
108	the better part of a year		150	with great skepticism
109	with the promise of		151	remind (someone) about
110	trace back to		152	twists and turns

153	disproportionately affects	195	twists and turns
154	lose the will to	196	all ability levels
155	failure to	197	on behalf of
156	it comes from	198	not necessarily
157	fail to	199	the fact that
158	a much larger role	200	experiencing delays
159	the cause of	201	the better part of a year
160	with the promise of	202	with great skepticism
161	remind (someone) about	203	due to damage to
162	is cancelled	204	leaning towards
163	complicit in	205	call in
164	driving to work	206	not the greatest
165	make a point	207	proven to be
166	traced back to	208	beat the clock
167	entitled to	209	like to go ahead
168	fill out	210	too vulgar
169	the idea of expressing	211	very different from
170	currently open	212	comes from
171	a victim of	213	preparing a meal
172	for the reason	214	chop vegetables
173	not necessarily	215	make good time
174	to solicit	216	linked to
175	counting the	217	to liaise with
176	sitting around a table	218	charged to
177	leave the house	219	based on
178	learn new	220	target for
179	in large part	221	a reflection of
180	enjoying (one's) meal	222	break into
181	to utilize	223	the preferences of
182	an analysis of	224	on the part of
183	get away with	225	almost all
184	lose the ability to	226	is not allowed
185	rein in	227	make an example of
186	working on	228	leave promptly at
187	run afoul of	229	meet with
188	fall short of	230	basic requirement
189	open up	231	wait for
190	back to	232	if you find
191	pleased to announce	233	which is tempting
192	make up for lost time	234	not hold water
193	mum's the word	235	not rocket science
194	nickel and dime someone (to death)	236	off the charts

STEP 92

Sentence Writing Practice - #2

Form sentences with each of the following to demonstrate your understanding.

1	take place	34	aid and abet
2	a defiant stance	35	delivered to
3	defiant attitude	36	business downturn
4	at the same level	37	news coverage
5	go sometime soon	38	comment on the letter
6	the fee for	39	does not take place
7	engulfed in	40	to speak at
8	in the mall	41	exact fare
9	train your efforts	42	need it before
10	assume office	43	the problem with
11	as big as	44	company was founded
12	assumption of office	45	challenge the status quo
13	more successful than	46	strictly prohibited
14	well organized	47	meet the needs of
15	towering figure	48	easy to get to
16	a scheduling conflict	49	explore new ways of
17	comes to	50	in the hospital
18	social security stipend	51	put the arm on someone
19	heavy smoker	52	go ahead
20	on speed dial	53	even though
21	poke fun	54	filthy trailer
22	announce the date	55	could afford
23	leading position	56	food-encrusted plates
24	full speed ahead	57	on our mission
25	try something different	58	our valued clients
26	lose control of	59	have to wait
27	reminded that	60	rule violations
28	after lunch	61	facing blowback
29	cede space	62	prepared by
30	cultural appropriation	63	stuck in traffic
31	quote, unquote	64	writ large
32	a rain check	65	raise the bar
33	wide off the mark	66	rant and rave

67	every now and then	109	take up to
68	not normal	110	required for
69	incredibly distasteful	111	take it back
70	offer perspective	112	for every item
71	take time off	113	step back
72	how else	114	how else
73	watching TV	115	bear witness
74	remind myself	116	should not do
75	whatever your reasons are	117	forget to
76	what i believe is	118	appear on
77	is aspirational	119	at least
78	accepted into	120	signing the document
79	all about	121	volunteer for
80	explaining a chart	122	to that extent
81	is a catalyst	123	left with
82	filing papers	124	open to
83	on the trip	125	proof of
84	different roles	126	occur to me
85	at most	127	simply to express
86	must be so offended	128	per night
87	as humanly possible	129	the type of room
88	confirm that	130	on the wall
89	suit (someone)	131	something problematic
90	flying a plane	132	reading a book
91	by being afraid	133	request in advance
92	costs an extra	134	shaking hands
93	get paid for	135	take it back
94	did not pull any punches	136	to document
95	catapult from	137	around the world
96	deign to assume	138	two blocks further than
97	against all odds	139	pleasant evening to
98	taking a nap	140	get the permission of
99	point the way	141	as a way to
100	in part because	142	through a garden
101	make an impression	143	on the side
102	as soon as possible	144	preparing dinner
103	able to	145	want to begin
104	carved out	146	gain notoriety
105	decide how	147	set of decisions
106	patient as Job	148	push someone's buttons
107	pay dividends	149	put something in a nutshell
108	point a finger at	150	put two and two together

151	experienced managers		193	commitment to unity
152	a round of		194	pay off
153	how far		195	feel as though
154	a reservation for		196	on the part of
155	what it is		197	a major drawback
156	there is no point		198	kind of hotel
157	agreed on		199	a great time to
158	it can take		200	turn to
159	use of the		201	made him famous
160	a feeling of safety		202	favorable to
161	on a shoestring		203	taking a call
162	good at		204	in tune with
163	approach		205	make the most of
164	more inappropriate		206	receive credit for
165	could care less		207	spend the most time on
166	concourse is empty		208	serious problems
167	couldn't care less		209	a newspaper subscription
168	plans for		210	can't emphasize enough
169	all the same size		211	couldn't agree more
170	examining a patient		212	review of
171	less on...and more on...		213	concluded from
172	spells trouble		214	return (someone's) course soon
173	before the move		215	included in
174	closely allied with		216	clear focus
175	fail to		217	a security system
176	it is best to		218	never considered
177	gain access to		219	in your home
178	done with care		220	address issues of
179	sufficient to		221	less frequently
180	less professional		222	resonance with
181	with no obligation		223	in any case
182	resonate with		224	a unifying message
183	continue to		225	attract attention
184	criticized by		226	begin on time
185	criticized for being		227	being offered
186	unwilling to		228	unable to
187	tired of getting up to		229	create havoc
188	significant advantages		230	respond to
189	adoption of		231	return from
190	on the fringe		232	out of character
191	on the wane		233	out of the woods
192	an open-and-shut case		234	par for the course

STEP 93

Sentence Writing Practice #3

Form sentences with each of the following to demonstrate your understanding.

#	Phrase	#	Phrase
1	take place	34	aid and abet
2	a defiant stance	35	delivered to
3	defiant attitude	36	business downturn
4	at the same level	37	news coverage
5	go sometime soon	38	comment on the letter
6	the fee for	39	does not take place
7	engulfed in	40	to speak at
8	in the mall	41	exact fare
9	train your efforts	42	need it before
10	assume office	43	the problem with
11	as big as	44	company was founded
12	assumption of office	45	challenge the status quo
13	more successful than	46	strictly prohibited
14	well organized	47	meet the needs of
15	towering figure	48	easy to get to
16	a scheduling conflict	49	explore new ways of
17	comes to	50	in the hospital
18	social security stipend	51	ready to roll
19	heavy smoker	52	go ahead
20	on speed dial	53	even though
21	poke fun	54	filthy trailer
22	announce the date	55	could afford
23	leading position	56	food-encrusted plates
24	full speed ahead	57	on our mission
25	try something different	58	our valued clients
26	lose control of	59	have to wait
27	reminded that	60	rule violations
28	after lunch	61	facing blowback
29	cede space	62	prepared by
30	cultural appropriation	63	stuck in traffic
31	a red herring	64	saddled with
32	resonate with someone	65	school of thought
33	rub elbows with	66	settle a score with

67	goals for	109	maximize the number of
68	fill in	110	much clearer
69	wearing glasses	111	start to refute
70	turn off	112	talk in circles
71	lean into controversy	113	interacting with
72	eerily quiet	114	during the conference
73	a perfect example	115	standing at a booth
74	having said that	116	not as good
75	spend my vacation	117	more procedural
76	completely riveting	118	reading the news
77	not invited	119	was not until
78	lulled into	120	taking care of
79	culture clash	121	steer the ship
80	a motive for	122	later stages
81	formal role	123	out sick
82	less professional	124	arrive on time
83	brokered by	125	overwhelmed by
84	at the behest of	126	take attention away from
85	some place warmer	127	fastest-growing
86	clear and defined	128	on a business trip
87	take a deep dive into	129	more efficient
88	right below	130	how it all came together
89	on a bridge	131	set the stage for
90	identifying problems	132	the harder thing to do
91	for more than	133	do so poorly
92	required qualifications	134	until now
93	a good amount	135	want to discuss at the meeting
94	rent a room	136	cover over
95	much lankier	137	allow free discussion
96	have a good trip	138	doted on by
97	best interest at hear	139	the one I prefer is
98	unbeknownst to her	140	focus on important matters
99	appreciate (someone's) interest in	141	the chemistry is such that
100	can be a little difficult	142	apply for the position of
101	much more nuanced	143	as morbid as it is
102	go over the plans	144	a terrific actor
103	project maturity	145	not as good
104	wish i had known	146	suit your needs
105	far more illuminating	147	good preparation for
106	step up to the plate	148	take a bath on something
107	stop on a dime	149	take someone for a ride
108	sweeten the pot	150	take shape

151	couldn't have had a more pleasant	193	across the street
152	utmost respect	194	strike a balance
153	why don't you	195	in debt
154	as nicely as possible	196	go awry
155	hope to	197	a healthful lunch
156	bilateral relationship	198	relative stability
157	full-throated	199	reserve a table
158	run a meeting	200	sports landscape
159	want to buy	201	take the brunt of
160	a quarter of	202	a shady deal
161	will come next week	203	fundamental to maintain
162	genuine perception	204	a sharp tongue
163	prefer to	205	next to the
164	coffee with milk	206	fill in
165	sanding the table	207	rules for
166	unpaid internship	208	waste time
167	air a new series	209	it is possible for
168	safety concerns	210	multiple reports
169	lose (one's) job	211	finger pointing
170	a great opportunity for	212	upcoming trip
171	clearest proof	213	get some practice
172	happy to meet with	214	overshadowed
173	not allowed	215	ahead of
174	a little differently	216	have more free time
175	use the priority seating area	217	growing exasperation
176	not available on	218	behind-the-scenes efforts
177	medical practice	219	on the defensive
178	apparently successful	220	the date you mentioned
179	nowhere to go but up	221	unusually reserved
180	not always popular	222	if you disagree
181	a pretext to	223	very far
182	as much as	224	make an appointment for
183	at risk	225	interested in accepting
184	on a daily basis	226	lack of transparency
185	boarding the train	227	given that
186	in the darkroom	228	a possible presentation
187	fuming about	229	the program lasts from
188	account for	230	sound off on
189	a little premature	231	widespread criticism
190	shoot from the hip	232	soft soap
191	sit on the fence	233	spare no expense
192	smoke and mirrors	234	split hairs

STEP 94

Sentence Writing Practice - #4

1	fighting back	37	over the past few weeks
2	in relation to	38	getting along with
3	call (someone) out	39	come under fire
4	enraged that	40	responsible for
5	seem to claim that	41	not mince words
6	selected based on	42	participating since
7	in all honesty	43	economic dividends
8	double standards	44	founding father
9	it is recommended to	45	in related fields
10	spread out	46	revisit their policy
11	as many people as possible	47	compared to
12	purpose of	48	respond to
13	relatively new	49	broke down
14	shut off	50	come over
15	whenever possible	51	pleasant atmosphere
16	turn it clockwise	52	sold out
17	important to	53	so fast
18	make a phone call	54	standard assessment
19	developed by	55	a reduction in
20	get up early	56	on the right
21	get there	57	a description of
22	carry the ball	58	unfamiliar with
23	really well	59	over here
24	rather hot	60	seek detail-oriented person
25	true sense of	61	should apply by
26	travel frequently	62	always losing
27	discuss how to	63	method of shipment
28	curious about	64	encourage (someone) to
29	in a macabre way	65	set of circumstances
30	comfortable with	66	lack of fear
31	enormously compelling	67	well aware of
32	every so often	68	tend to be looking for
33	tickle the ivories	69	under a cloud (of suspicion)
34	toe the line	70	up in the air
35	touch and go	71	wait for the other shoe to drop
36	tread water	72	warm body

73	earn a living	116	at least
74	in the habit of	117	feel privileged
75	pan out	118	to work on
76	stir the pot	119	diplomatic way of
77	try and choose	120	to work on
78	perfectly happy	121	all the time
79	in the short time since	122	it happened a few days of each other
80	deliberative process	123	always have
81	frame of reference	124	a great deal of
82	a life of	125	a rare moment
83	deal with	126	ended up
84	in the short term	127	on the margins
85	go it alone	128	is an indication of
86	ten years of experience	129	very bad in there
87	the meeting starts	130	foreseeable future
88	asleep in	131	more active
89	somewhat complimentary	132	allocate funds
90	not specialized	133	still not convinced
91	talk to	134	the repairs will take
92	pretty surprised	135	really cheap
93	a bit strange	136	all aboard
94	awake at	137	spar with
95	provide (someone) with	138	went on the wrong date
96	the deadline for	139	make a mistake
97	shipped to	140	strong enough
98	unfettered authority	141	cheer loudly
99	will be painted	142	big enough
100	one of the most outrageous	143	an extremely small
101	a pretty big	144	a really big
102	wrong with	145	fairly high
103	quite high	146	so high that
104	too high for	147	in an attempt to
105	hear a conversation between	148	as high as
106	how high	149	higher than
107	went on the wrong date	150	sit at a desk
108	achieve substantive goals	151	approximately 50% of
109	hear the phone	152	stand up to
110	gain the confidence	153	extremely small
111	bring to light	154	completely dry
112	walk on eggshells	155	at one's fingertips
113	white collar	156	all walks of life
114	zero in on	157	be my guest
115	all or nothing	158	in detention

159	absolutely full		201	a complete disorder
160	appear before		202	the diagram shown
161	an extremely cold		203	moderately cold
162	always late		204	certain that
163	very particular		205	quite right
164	quite difference		206	quite hungry
165	enfeebled state		207	everyone is welcome
166	quite cold		208	necessary ingredients
167	full mastery of		209	an open window
168	almost possible		210	existing facilities
169	a very stressful job		211	during the summer holidays
170	a nearby restaurant		212	claim to be in touch with
171	received mail		213	waited outside
172	received a letter		214	the older generation
173	for ages		215	in my desk
174	what kind of room		216	on my desk
175	itching to		217	quickly realized
176	started to		218	in the soup
177	constant critic		219	by no means
178	live up to		220	still to do
179	next big issue		221	ask for
180	to ascertain		222	lose a lot of weight
181	not only necessary but possible		223	by all accounts
182	successfully achieve		224	an open question
183	how stunning		225	clash of ideas
184	a cold enough		226	those who use
185	out of the office		227	little else
186	influence an argument		228	repaint the car
187	asking for		229	safety considerations
188	research facilities		230	crowded with
189	better off than		231	overdraw an account
190	open for election		232	exhausted by
191	withhold support		233	all day
192	best bet		234	how long does it take to get to
193	supposed to be		235	pushing the pram
194	deeply sad		236	in her early 30s
195	what is wrong with		237	plan new products
196	eviction notice		238	shake one's head no
197	through a marketing network		239	opt for
198	short-term gain		240	clear and convincing evidence
199	preoccupied with		241	a giant step
200	completely bogus		242	put the lie to

STEP 95

Sentence Writing Practice - #5

Form sentences with each of the following to demonstrate your understanding.

1	regardless of	34	becoming increasingly popular
2	doing some planning	35	hint at the possibility
3	intractable issue	36	through the media
4	in the meadow	37	save the environment
5	impartial justice	38	strewn on the streets
6	have a quick lunch	39	internally inconsistent
7	mention the date of	40	get hold of
8	reverse the trend	41	denied the charge
9	remain anonymous	42	looked strange
10	get started planning	43	view x with suspicion
11	emphasis is on	44	the construction of
12	elegant solutions	45	increasing rapidly
13	intutitive appeal	46	around the hostel
14	inversion of	47	enviable skill
15	find out why	48	surveyed about
16	make up	49	tinker with
17	provide (someone) with	50	on the table
18	very relaxing	51	about to learn
19	at the controls	52	speculated that
20	built on	53	currently affecting
21	so proud of	54	help expose
22	marketing gimmick	55	delivered the sealed bid
23	convene a meeting	56	constant encouragement
24	all contribute to	57	more hazardous than
25	from all over the world	58	the extent of
26	relentless practicality	59	open too early
27	to provide misconduct	60	hiring good employees
28	clamp down on	61	wise choice environmentally
29	seem large	62	too closely relate
30	move in tandem	63	flight is delayed
31	do a delicate dance	64	rage against
32	sore at (someone)	65	politically motivated
33	low level of loyalty	66	tighten the noose around

67	by any means	109	don't have enough time
68	trying to finalize	110	marred by
69	expect to attend	111	how to get to
70	grappling with	112	attract attention
71	appear adrift	113	at the helm
72	a blow to	114	neglect of
73	consumer trends	115	have (someone) do
74	expect to find	116	another path
75	go off the rails	117	purchase of
76	her chosen field	118	minor problems
77	taxes are included	119	tendency to dismiss
78	pleased to announce	120	when (someone) is due in (a city)
79	in the periphery	121	for a brief time
80	gain notoriety	122	leave it with
81	existential crisis	123	go undetected
82	limiting exploration	124	a new sort of
83	easy to find	125	expressive person
84	proceed with	126	not only that
85	what was more	127	fascinated by
86	yet-unnamed	128	build on
87	would be	129	intentionally deceptive
88	muddy the waters	130	in keeping with
89	cordially invite	131	revived interest
90	utter falsehood	132	it is important to use
91	lose customers	133	not totally sure
92	cases of misconduct	134	profited from
93	bring light to	135	used in research
94	served by	136	want to finalize
95	draw the interest of	137	increasingly acting like
96	a more transparent course of action	138	more shops across the country
97	point of view	139	from this perspective
98	determine the cost	140	as long as
99	dangerously complacent	141	a new line of
100	currently being investigated	142	sort of products
101	a minor concern	143	expressions of concern
102	serious harm	144	likely to attend
103	more efficient than	145	have a connecting flight to
104	strewn across	146	it seems essential
105	invested in	147	the person who
106	at a detriment	148	quite divergent from
107	firm disapproval	149	line of thinking
108	unfairly scrutinized	150	what can be done

151	a multitude of ways	193	holds true
152	deliberate misconduct	194	after (one) disembarks
153	conceal key facts	195	in search of
154	soon after	196	needlessly fraught
155	from one area	197	to try to influence
156	little motivation	198	not illegal to
157	do for	199	until (one) sees
158	due by	200	emerge from
159	sort through	201	had a resurgence
160	versatile enough	202	a new revelation
161	the latest equipment	203	conceal key facts
162	in recent years	204	the variety of
163	narrow down	205	join a seminar
164	a handful of	206	have dinner with
165	aware that	207	what constitutes
166	overrule the advice of	208	distinguish a from b
167	express my heartfelt gratitude	209	never go out of style
168	using it for	210	not in service
169	much success to	211	get a discount
170	daily briefing	212	it would seem
171	deal with the theme of	213	a dismally small sample
172	new production techniques	214	open to new ideas
173	did better than	215	in the hands of
174	realize that	216	feel like
175	listen well	217	the itinerary is filed with
176	expect to cut	218	secretive culture
177	increasingly uneasy	219	in collaboration with
178	how do you want to	220	wonderful reviews
179	pension plan	221	a troop of actors
180	similar themes	222	government regulations
181	post a closing notice	223	a disservice to
182	money-losing project	224	independent of
183	show it to	225	for the first time
184	the world at large	226	see a progression in
185	supportive of	227	starting wage
186	brought to you by	228	check in for
187	reduction in the labor force	229	crack the code
188	as you well know	230	blamed for
189	take pride in	231	for a long time
190	point a way forward	232	all but admit
191	what is needed to	233	have no knowledge of
192	still not decided	234	diametrically opposed

STEP 96

Sentence Writing Practice - #6

1	on the kerb	37	controversial policy
2	walking downstairs	38	flip on
3	smell of	39	eating right
4	how often does	40	reach over
5	walking upstairs	41	step into
6	strung from	42	dimly lit
7	a benefit of	43	stay above
8	need assistance with	44	where to begin
9	ride it out	45	walk in circles
10	safety issues	46	holler back
11	encouraged to	47	substandard home
12	if you stay on	48	under risky terms
13	targeted by	49	reassure employees
14	the store carries	50	should arrive in
15	talked into	51	a major change
16	cut back	52	grinding lenses
17	take out	53	lured into
18	on the porch	54	announce an expansion
19	speedy recovery	55	methodical way
20	dishevelled office	56	slovenly ways
21	try to help	57	how often do
22	try not to step on	58	previous home
23	start in on	59	lurch away
24	beeping sounds	60	sent under separate cover
25	reduce opportunity for	61	wander through
26	set at a comfortable level	62	in a matter of hours
27	climb out of	63	make (something) safe
28	retire from	64	bear down on
29	a wave of questions	65	a real inspiration for
30	sell tickets for	66	say with great confidence
31	being undone	67	wild allegation
32	pull into	68	incumbent upon
33	flying time will be	69	highly doubt
34	encircled in	70	protracted process
35	arriving at the office	71	make a crack at
36	participate in	72	fair warning

73	up close	115	make room for
74	woke up to find	116	reprimanded by
75	call back	117	depend on (someone) for advice
76	over and over again	118	root out
77	go far deeper	119	at the day's end
78	default arrangement	120	watching a parade
79	muffled scream	121	in the dumps
80	end up	122	use the enclosed envelope
81	the fate of	123	kind of training
82	incorrect calculations	124	undermined by
83	new for of scrutiny	125	turn off the lights
84	more like	126	rounding error
85	stand for	127	hiring freeze
86	feeling rattled	128	turn out to be
87	reports of turbulence	129	the brainchild of
88	with respect to	130	talk passion
89	unauthorized	131	is offered
90	be heard	132	self-appointed
91	a cruising altitude of	133	portend a future in which
92	a valuable contribution	134	entering an office
93	promise to correct an error	135	manage the budget
94	scientific fraud	136	except for
95	persuade (someone) to	137	the publicity about
96	only a handful of	138	is always available
97	spark uproar	139	help improve
98	reduce water usage	140	look out on to
99	the destination for	141	of her own devising
100	leave promptly	142	as we know it
101	show off	143	much more serious
102	meet (someone) at	144	keep a sharp eye
103	release from	145	have had to leave
104	expected to be	146	earnest about
105	see progress	147	suggested organizing
106	more prevalent	148	growth will come
107	would appreciate it if	149	sensitive territory
108	more current than	150	given for
109	mutual trust	151	weary grin
110	next decade	152	a spate of
111	on multiple fronts	153	bipartisan consensus
112	abuse of power	154	in a crude sense
113	too vital a tool	155	express dissatisfaction
114	a grave abuse	156	the defining element

157	empty the wastebasket		199	asking for help
158	on the forefront		200	increase awareness of
159	a reservation for		201	will be announced
160	inundated by		202	review emergency procedures
161	more expensive than		203	at the same time
162	observe that		204	download a file
163	crude estimates		205	two decades later
164	meet new people		206	raise rates
165	collate the results		207	under the desk
166	given to		208	about to start
167	purely rational		209	akin to
168	apt comparison		210	cutting through
169	watch the game		211	will be seated
170	receiving award		212	keep others from
171	retracted article		213	express dissatisfaction
172	give (someone) a ride		214	mid-sized business
173	very large		215	even closer together
174	very surprised		216	must be mailed out
175	the majority of		217	the result of
176	upload a file		218	looking into
177	learning to navigate		219	cannot send
178	seems likely		220	sales skills
179	depended on		221	a few of the suggested
180	especially popular		222	a protest over
181	plug a hole		223	within a week of
182	asked to do		224	no one knows better than
183	quality of products		225	how devastating
184	discover why		226	regard as
185	indicates that		227	nudge (something) along
186	the vast majority		228	self-reporting
187	unlikely place		229	meet again
188	can't seem to find the time		230	unnoticed but significant ways
189	prestigious journal		231	please realize that
190	easy command of		232	seemingly trivial matter
191	some of our new items		233	contracts are ready
192	visible minorities		234	a promising scientist
193	leaving the harbor		235	in small quantities
194	vein of thought		236	wasteful habits
195	third shift		237	a knack for
196	turn on (someone)		238	remain relevant
197	unusually harsh		239	a key feature
198	out to get (someone)		240	gain a sense of

STEP 97

Sentence Writing Practice - #7

#	Phrase	#	Phrase
1	staggeringly small	37	being sensitive to
2	exceeded x's expectations	38	train bound for
3	have creative autonomy	39	in any facet of
4	less apt to	40	remember something
5	began to realize	41	the close of business today
6	rules of contribution	42	working with clients
7	all-inclusive hot springs	43	call back during
8	in conversation with	44	place the blame on
9	gender disparities	45	not afraid to try
10	a different view of	46	into action
11	visual reference	47	not afraid of
12	eligible to receive	48	see echoes of
13	great to see	49	an urgency to
14	doing irreparable harm	50	that resonates with
15	no experience is required	51	a serious subject
16	contact X	52	necessary reforms
17	as part of the package	53	when it comes to
18	at the center of	54	a real melange
19	an important story to tell	55	true story of
20	an enormous amount of	56	brimming with
21	carve out	57	it is expected that
22	care about	58	felt as though
23	a turbulent journey	59	using better technology
24	continue to evolve	60	fall in love with
25	in those hiatuses	61	finding material
26	have a positive effect on	62	importance of
27	push back	63	becoming popular
28	a pertinent subject	64	the premier name in
29	pretty consistently	65	a conversation piece
30	compared with	66	entrenched position
31	span a larger period	67	for all practical purposes
32	prior to	68	far later than
33	broadly speaking	69	thousands of pages
34	as it is perceived	70	on the promise of
35	in the landscape	71	incriminating information
36	show up at	72	with the explicit intention of

73	coming forward	115	expected to be
74	health coverage	116	a local landmark
75	an unfavorable view of	117	rolled out
76	the purpose of	118	influence over
77	unalterably opposed	119	something quieter
78	up to date	120	environmentally responsible manner
79	issued every month	121	it is imperative that
80	keep an office running	122	vehemently opposed to
81	the only thing	123	able to reach
82	bogged down	124	especially tragic
83	toll-free number	125	insist that
84	with regard to	126	told (someone) to leave by
85	except in emergencies	127	create misunderstanding
86	over the long term	128	translate into
87	sorry to hear	129	the stakes are very high
88	reaping the fruits	130	leave the place at
89	reduce costs	131	from the very beginning
90	it seems to be .	132	particularly sad
91	put on hold	133	feel boxed in
92	a great dea of	134	could not figure out
93	hoping against hope that	135	submit ideas to
94	generous support of	136	put one's cards on the table
95	take center stage	137	invited to board
96	with bated breath	138	as of this morning
97	in keeping with	139	an open question
98	there is a lot of damage to	140	do things differently
99	gone to lunch	141	punch back
100	the seriousness of the case	142	clearly a provocation
101	is listed	143	will no longer be
102	cover a variety of	144	the current arrangement
103	continue through the weekend	145	keep others from
104	impinge upon	146	with grace
105	convergence of	147	cease production
106	an open question	148	learn about
107	satisfaction in	149	on average
108	too large or too small	150	ability to meet
109	extremely worried	151	in addition to
110	protesting against	152	call for advice about
111	try to influence	153	absolutely fascinating
112	interfered to help	154	request a meeting
113	similar capabilities	155	run amok
114	isolated from	156	imminent action

157	nature of preferential options	199	work best if
158	bag of hot air	200	quickly became clear that
159	have some suggestions for	201	operate on a weekend schedule
160	possible ties to	202	catch up on
161	a meeting with	203	recovering at a clinic
162	dig into	204	move forward
163	looking toward	205	regret to announce that
164	point of departure	206	prelude to
165	as readily available as necessary	207	that led to
166	the directory lists	208	make sure
167	thorough instruction	209	lose ground
168	go through the roof	210	upset with
169	tangled in a web of	211	perpetrated on
170	until further notice	212	do (something) well
171	tender one's resignation	213	by the end of the year
172	badly injured	214	provide opportunities
173	deserve to be	215	hang on the wall
174	pay on average	216	come close
175	working the phones	217	to break promises
176	too much already	218	tackle taxes
177	in and of itself	219	plain language
178	no longer required to	220	keep one's word
179	freedom to	221	final measure
180	make (something) clear	222	address concerns
181	yet again	223	immune from outrage
182	leave your belongings	224	exercise (one's) own judgment
183	as a replacement	225	give assurances
184	ace in (someone's) pocket	226	get pared down
185	become law	227	further an agenda
186	friction between	228	gaining control
187	become increasingly convinced	229	need to be available to
188	finely-tuned machine	230	going to try
189	subtle understanding	231	do not include
190	choice words for	232	transportation option
191	to develop new products	233	not relevant to
192	during special periods	234	get off the phone
193	return (someone's) call	235	refer to
194	the real reason	236	update training
195	on track	237	financial disclosure
196	excellent indication	238	imprimatur of credibility
197	familiar faces	239	a potential role
198	look the part	240	on the rocks

STEP 98

Sentence Writing Practice - #8

#	Phrase	#	Phrase
1	save on costs	37	make a reservation
2	point out issues	38	make changes
3	on the record	39	the potential discount on
4	from public sources	40	necessary to get help
5	composed of	41	key problem
6	reject (something) out of hand	42	in honor of
7	tepid apology	43	keep one's word
8	routine work	44	come close
9	subsidized day care	45	tender one's resignation
10	deserve to be	46	does not mince words
11	by the end of the year	47	travel between A and B
12	transported by trucks	48	the handbook explains
13	come from the well	49	perpetrated on
14	a series of	50	safe flight
15	backed up by	51	personal rapport
16	didn't realize that	52	obsessed with
17	donate profits to	53	offensive to
18	not unexpected	54	no good options
19	further proof of	55	swift retaliation
20	restrict the use of	56	send a strong message
21	acting contrary to	57	impose sanctions on
22	earn a salary	58	becoming more open
23	emblematic of	59	a direct response
24	a record of complaints is	60	absent from
25	lower the cost of	61	referred to as
26	terribly slow	62	leading position
27	full speed ahead	63	cede space
28	our valued clients	64	rule violations
29	as outlined by	65	lose control of
30	facing blowback	66	it is advisable to
31	nobody will be available to	67	review the contract
32	the only difference between A and B	68	enraged that
33	lack of due diligence	69	hard to believe
34	postponement of the process	70	sing someone's praises
35	cast aside	71	an important point
36	concern runs deep	72	have a change of heart

73	take on	115	can't help but
74	what I think	116	waiting to order
75	an early appointment	117	members must have
76	pan out	118	strong desire
77	it happened a few days of each other	119	include free
78	a life of	120	labor assistance
79	frame of reference	121	at least
80	a great deal of	122	feel privileged
81	always have	123	in the habit of
82	deliberative process	124	to work on
83	deal with	125	stir the pot
84	leave in half an hour	126	to work on
85	ended up	127	try and choose
86	in the short term	128	diplomatic way of
87	in the short time since	129	all the time
88	submit your appeal within	130	perfectly happy
89	earn a living	131	the best it possibly can be
90	must be accompanied by	132	to stand up to
91	is an indication of	133	foreseeable future
92	taste test	134	feel numb
93	extremely small	135	pretty surprised
94	fulfill (one's) duties	136	all aboard
95	how high	137	awake at
96	higher than	138	as high as
97	more active	139	a bit strange
98	not specialized	140	asleep in
99	somewhat complimentary	141	a really big
100	have been planning	142	a pretty big
101	really cheap	143	time to get up
102	on the margins	144	strong enough
103	still not convinced	145	big enough
104	go it alone	146	come under scrutiny
105	completely dry	147	gain the confidence
106	initiate the following	148	so high that
107	too high for	149	quite high
108	absolutely full	150	fairly high
109	almost possible	151	very particular
110	certain that	152	always late
111	based on (one's) experience	153	on the business front
112	head for the exit	154	in one's eagerness
113	in the next few months	155	much was made of
114	long-standing relationship	156	unusual bond

157	an extremely small		199	quite cold
158	quite right		200	have already bought
159	quite hungry		201	no parking zone
160	moderately cold		202	a complete disorder
161	due to unforeseen circumstances		203	corrode support for
162	everyone is welcome		204	an open window
163	necessary ingredients		205	a very stressful job
164	a nearby restaurant		206	appear before
165	for too long		207	an extremely cold
166	was starving		208	constant critic
167	the diagram shown		209	by no means
168	the older generation		210	by all accounts
169	in the soup		211	live up to
170	started to		212	still to do
171	quickly realized		213	next big issue
172	on my desk		214	itching to
173	in my desk		215	not only necessary but possible
174	waited outside		216	for ages
175	clash of ideas		217	hospitalized for
176	an open question		218	how stunning
177	a number of priorities		219	would not bother
178	represent a change		220	obliged to do
179	submit a report		221	to ascertain
180	honor the contract		222	those who use
181	a cold enough		223	agreed upon by
182	a calculation of		224	customer-parking limit
183	what is unusual about		225	approaching rapidly
184	a check written out to		226	make frequent trips
185	sign the addendum to the contract		227	reference letter
186	stretched to the limit		228	pay in person
187	never laughed so hard		229	knock on the door
188	ticket number		230	state the reason
189	scattered throughout		231	don't forget to ask
190	take advantage of		232	definitely been finished
191	stuffed with down		233	there's no reason to
192	will be delayed		234	take advantage of
193	unable to say		235	all your needs
194	offer top quality		236	go through customs
195	turn the page		237	paying too much
196	give concessions		238	translate A into B
197	nice way of putting (something)		239	stunning feat
198	incumbent on		240	swell of excitement

STEP 99

Sentence Writing Practice - #9

1	work slowdown	37	an alert has been issued
2	sometime last week	38	enclosing a money order
3	wipe the table	39	pleased to receive
4	get more information	40	broadly speaking
5	the first step in	41	to send the invoice
6	maneuver through	42	deathly afraid of
7	take to storage	43	victimized by
8	should not be necessary	44	ramp up
9	disgusting spot	45	come under fire
10	eager to	46	will be held
11	pleased to receive	47	will be held in
12	scratched-up furniture	48	does not mince words
13	per pallet per month	49	in all honesty
14	in the safe	50	economic dividends
15	find a way	51	revisit their policy
16	take up	52	at the bottom of
17	have trouble with	53	free shuttle service
18	without a doubt	54	a bit too expensive
19	with the advent of	55	relatively new
20	just about to	56	suggest ways for
21	can't help but	57	from each branch
22	a strong desire to	58	come back bigger
23	better products	59	struggling to stay afloat
24	it"s hard to discern	60	play host to
25	looking for	61	express optimism
26	take on	62	watch out for
27	what I think	63	criminal investigation
28	such a hassle	64	put something to bed
29	a complete walk back	65	suffer in silence
30	suggest keeping	66	at its core
31	wall off	67	at the initiative of
32	down is up	68	get rid of
33	with a parting shot	69	address concerns
34	genuine joy	70	at full tilt
35	see eye to eye on	71	seem receptive to
36	rule out the possibility of	72	stick to one's guns

73	on the cusp of	115	give (someone) an out
74	there's no question that	116	a controversial policy
75	aiding and abetting	117	step aside from
76	rip up (something)	118	stay and fight
77	a temporary remedy	119	as yet unproven
78	keep one's eyes wide open	120	be caught by surprise
79	less cynical	121	numerous allegations
80	learn more about	122	bang on the door
81	improve upon	123	put one's job on the line
82	how much weight to put on	124	lack of experience
83	as recently as	125	undergo vetting
84	take real issue with	126	proven facts
85	what's interesting is	127	laudatory about
86	by the end of	128	glowing reviews
87	a detriment to	129	particularly unusial
88	swing vote	130	much less likely
89	keep something at bay	131	need to know more
90	have the right to	132	give a window into
91	dig into	133	lay it all out
92	a big step back	134	get something resolved
93	rotten to the core	135	count on (someone)
94	stay in place	136	particular problem
95	critically important issue	137	take a quick break
96	cannot get anything done	138	the big issue is
97	nothing has been done	139	host of questions
98	in the last few months	140	more details about
99	get a reprieve	141	passed out drunk
100	dereliction of duty	142	prescribe medications
101	excessive drinking	143	raise the stakes
102	stand by (someone)	144	strains credulity
103	facing serious questions	145	abundant resources
104	not dropping out	146	allegations of impropriety
105	odds are stacked against	147	minutes from now
106	doesn't have any choice	148	seeking to reschedule
107	what's frustrating	149	circling the wagons
108	continue to find	150	had it up to here with (someone)
109	step away from	151	fired off a memo
110	pull out of	152	open to the possibility of
111	work with (someone)	153	made its way to
112	far from perfect	154	denigrating comments
113	take blame for	155	what emerges is
114	thoroughly vetted	156	get to the nitty-gritty

157	extraordinarily broad	199	in recent weeks
158	in regards to	200	a fraught position
159	not in a position to	201	true to oneself
160	what's behind that	202	a flawed strategy
161	complete and accurate	203	pull something off
162	curious about	204	cement a relationship
163	the first piece	205	have someone in one's corner
164	in essence	206	close the door on something
165	come as no surprise to	207	make no progress
166	for a couple of reasons	208	out of control
167	what if anything	209	look worried
168	question (one's) motives	210	running out of time
169	information sufficient to	211	sink deeper and deeper into trouble
170	for reasons that make sense	212	couldn't be stopped by
171	put (someone) on the horns of a dilemma	213	desperately trying to
172	an unusual step	214	just how frazzled
173	an overriding public interest	215	want a seat at the table
174	the least damaging damage	216	ahead of one's time
175	not in a position to	217	it mystifies me that
176	what's behind that...	218	out of the shadows
177	complete and accurate	219	as far as I can tell
178	curious about	220	deciding exactly when
179	the first piece	221	significant debt of gratitude
180	in essence	222	look askance at
181	come as no surprise to	223	see eye to eye
182	for a couple of reasons	224	serious concerns
183	question your motives	225	inappropriate manner
184	information sufficient to	226	inspire jealousy
185	for reasons that make sense	227	abusive relationship
186	elicit a response	228	evolving story
187	in the long run	229	the most difficult situation
188	as best I can tell	230	at some point
189	a series of assertions	231	in the interest of
190	if there is a pause	232	truly believing
191	of a similar nature	233	get past something
192	the mark of a great leader	234	on the way home
193	for two reasons	235	without exception
194	get at the truth	236	at the graveside
195	one of the major pillars of	237	must have repeated
196	under attack	238	overtaken by exhaustion
197	lay siege to	239	have no memory of
198	no matter my concerns	240	pick up details

STEP 100

Sentence Writing Practice - #10

#	Phrase	#	Phrase
1	too offhand	36	a naive optimist
2	more commonly known as	37	inexorable progress
3	attempt to make sense of	38	a much better world
4	if only for	39	improve over time
5	within sight of	40	live to see
6	the critical event	41	suffer a setback
7	what would happen	42	the rule of law
8	the next logical step	43	brought under control
9	straighten out	44	widespread adoption of
10	in my mind	45	in recent decades
11	occurred to me	46	increasingly morose
12	have no memory of	47	morbid interest
13	propelled by	48	if it bleeds, it leads
14	waiting in line	49	beyond hope for
15	in the reception area	50	in the hope that
16	time to deal with	51	human efforts
17	want to remember	52	in their turn
18	the difference between A and B	53	problems to be solved
19	point out that	54	acute question
20	give advance warning	55	every aspect of
21	a few days short of	56	leave someone cold
22	in each instance	57	artistic flair
23	inability to share	58	in constant jeopardy
24	at a remove from	59	outstanding stupidity
25	stand in line	60	augmented by
26	in no way prepared to accept	61	peace and prosperity
27	rise to the occasion	62	yet to be conceived
28	steel oneself	63	no limit to
29	no way of knowing	64	not just another
30	relentless succession of	65	deeply personal reasons
31	on the horizon	66	poor governance
32	find meaning in	67	it is disheartening to see that
33	financial responsibility	68	in perpetual need of
34	plan of action	69	ground breaking research
35	for any reason	70	part of a program

71	buy into the idea of	113	off-color jokes
72	empower someone to	114	go berserk
73	find a way to	115	speak bluntly
74	know very little about	116	go a little further
75	a very difficult task	117	do not feel the same way
76	half a dozen	118	get even with
77	offer more opportunities	119	in the real world
78	the tables are beginning to turn	120	make fun of
79	long to see	121	less comfortable with
80	high quality education	122	more awkward
81	just keep growing	123	come out in defense of
82	tiny details	124	unwilling to do
83	hunting for (something)	125	selective outrage
84	surrounded by mystery	126	absolutely sublime
85	in a handful of	127	attacking hypocrisy
86	a little bit of support	128	not so perceptive
87	specifically looking for	129	not debatable
88	intrigued by	130	cross the line
89	fall in love with	131	a flattering appearance
90	where it came from	132	every single person
91	save from oblivion	133	express regret
92	an outlet for	134	go off the rails
93	at their disposal	135	run interference for
94	forgotten treasures	136	in a coma
95	at the heart of	137	corporate sponsor
96	give something a second life	138	improve quite a bit
97	in a special way	139	take ownership of
98	the same place	140	appreciation for
99	live without	141	break ground on
100	feel hopeful	142	fists flying
101	follow through	143	a moment of frustration
102	excluded from	144	release a statement
103	a housing crisis	145	a direct result of
104	go a long way	146	an amazing life
105	nowhere near	147	how disappointing that
106	a detailed portrait of	148	break the status quo
107	take on a project	149	sneak peek
108	demand improvement	150	brave enough
109	turn violent	151	after the curtain goes down
110	spark controversy	152	out of control
111	explain the disconnect	153	stand up against
112	a total disaster	154	do a splendid job of

155	be dead serious		197	regular commentator
156	call (someone) out		198	feel attached to
157	break the law		199	for our purposes
158	a mean thing to say		200	unexpected victory
159	good reminder		201	perceived deficiency
160	storm out		202	a big part of
161	common ground		203	a repudiation of
162	fair criticism		204	a sense of desperation
163	a lame defense		305	up to the mark
164	spark controversy		206	a cultural dimension
165	deeply value (something / someone)		207	a sense of identity
166	close loopholes		208	in response to
167	for the safety of		209	a cultural dimension
168	if and where		210	too aggressive
169	a common thread		211	toy with
170	see (something) in advance		212	make a trenchant case
171	give a preview of		213	have the luxury of
172	pin the blame on		214	without referring to
173	seem suspicious		215	reinvigoration of
174	classified information		216	with disdain
175	barely scratch the surface of		217	reasonably competent
176	spend more time with		218	astonishingly limited
177	at peace with		219	rail against
178	bargain with		220	rear its ugly head
179	blow the lid off		221	whittle down
180	running very smoothly		222	precision tool
181	only half kidding		223	at a disadvantage
182	without incident		224	direct (someone) to
183	pretending to be		225	a useful reminder
184	common commitment		226	come to relish
185	make a distinction between A and B		227	fall into disuse
186	that way lies...		228	persistent problem
187	a tiny proportion		229	trespass on
188	try to make		230	bear a resemblance to
189	a history of domination		231	terribly betrayed
190	inwardly-looking		232	seem to be very reluctant
191	tumble into		233	a widespread supposition
192	emphasis on plurality		234	a stubborn problem
193	mutual understanding		235	totally disagree with
194	be in the same boat		236	unfamiliar with
195	go it alone		237	the underbelly of
196	highly qualified		238	immensely important

About the Author

Everett Ofori holds an MBA from Heriot-Watt University (Scotland, UK) and a Master of Science, Finance, from the College for Financial Planning, Colorado, USA. He teaches Public Speaking, Management, Marketing, and English for Specific Purposes (Business Writing, Medical Writing, Meeting Facilitation, etc.). Everett has helped hundreds of high school and university students around the world to improve their writing and grades. He has also worked extensively with business executives (including those at the C-level).

Everett has worked with clients/students from the following organizations and more:

• Accenture	• Actelion
• Asahi Kasei Medical	• Asahi Soft Drink Research, Moriya
• Astellas	• Barclays
• Becton Dickinson	• Chugai/Roche Pharmaceuticals
• Disney	• ExxonMobil
• Fujitsu	• Goldman Sachs
• Gyao (Yahoo Japan)	• Hitachi Design
• IIJ (Internet Initiative Japan)	• Johnson & Johnson (Janssen)
• McKinsey Japan	• Mitsubishi (Shoji)
• Moody's	• National Institute of Land and Infrastructure Management, Tsukuba, Japan (NILIM)
• Orix	• PriceWaterhouseCoopers (PWC)
• Recruit	• Sekizenkai Nursing School, Soga, Kanagawa
• Sumisho	• Summit Agro International
• Sumitomo	• Suntory
• Tokyo International Business College, Asakusabashi, Tokyo	• Yokohama Child Welfare College (Hoiku Fukushi), Higashi Totsuka, Kanagawa

Notes

www.ingramcontent.com/pod-product-compliance
Lightning Source LLC
Chambersburg PA
CBHW080020110526
44587CB00021BA/3418